OIL PAINTING

John Holden

GALLERY BOOKS
An Imprint of W. H. Smith Publishers Inc.
112 Madison Avenue
New York City 10016

John Holden

Edited by Yvonne Deutch
Designed and illustrated by Elizabeth Rose
Picture research by Julia Wood

Published by
GALLERY BOOKS
An imprint of W.H. Smith Publishers Inc.
112 Madison Avenue, New York,
New York 10016

ISBN 0 8317 6563-1

Printed and bound in Italy by L.E.G.O.

Contents

Acknowledgements

Museum Boymans-Van Beuningen, Rotterdam: 43. Cooper Bridgeman Library: 6 (Phillips Collection, Washington), 52 (Musée Grenoble). Foundation E. G. Bührle Collection: 97B. Bulloz: 96TL (Louvre). City Art Galleries, Manchester: 27, 85. Courtauld Institute Galleries, London: 28, 89. Edinburgh University Press: 47 (Private Collection). Robert Fraser Gallery, London: 127. Giraudon: 7TR (Musée Basle), 12 (Ishibashi Collection, Tokyo), 35 (Musée Royaux des Beaux-Arts, Brussels), 61 (Louvre), 72 (Louvre), 96BL & TR (Louvre), 97TR (Philadelphia Museum of Modern Art), 102 (Louvre). Hirshhorn Museum & Sculpture Garden, Smithsonian Institution: 109. Michael Holford Library: 7L (Tate Gallery), 13TL (National Gallery, London), 34 (Louvre), 81 (Ginette Signac Collection), 82 (Bradford City Art Gallery), 125 (Tate Gallery). Sidney Janis Gallery, New York: 44 (Max Wesserman Collection, Massachusetts). Felix Klee Collection, Berne: 118. Courtesy of the Knoedler Gallery, London: 9TR, 31. Kunsthistorische Museum, Vienna: 70. Mas: III (Toledo Cathedral). Frederico Arborio Mella: 93 (Palacio de Liria, Prado). Cliche Musée Nationaux, Paris: 50 (Musée National d'Art Moderne), 58 (Louvre), 65 (Louvre), 92 (Louvre), 105 (Musée National d'Art Moderne). Museo Civico di Torino: 113. Museum of Modern Art, New York: 106. Courtesy of the Trustees, National Gallery, London: 1 (photo: John Freeman), 2, 3, 13TL, 42, 90. National Gallery of Art, Washington D.C. 41 (Chester Dale Collection), 115 (on loan, Collection of the Artist). Neue Gallerie Sammlung Ludwig, Aachen: 10. Kunnstamlinger, Oslo Kommunes: 23. Roger Phillips: 45. Pucciarelli: 114 (Luigi dei Francesci, Rome), 119BR. Rowan Gallery: 37, 117. Scala: 5 (Musée Beaux-Arts, Reims), 13BR (Monaco Germania Neuepinakothek), 95 (Museum of Modern Art, Barcelona). Scottish National Gallery of Modern Art: 15, 53. Snark International: 8 (Albright Knox Gallery, Buffalo), 18 (Musée Toulouse-Lautrec, Albi), 40 (National d'Art Moderne, Paris). Städelsches Kunstinstitut, Frankfurt: 62. Stedelijk Museum, Amsterdam: 69. Trustees of the Tate Gallery, London: 4, 7L, 9B, 46, 55 (photo: John Webb), 57, 80, 103, 104 (photo: John Webb), 108, 109, 112, 125. Rodney Todd-White: 49, 94, 110. Jerry Tubby: 122. Victoria and Albert Museum, London, Crown Copyright: 64. Waddington and Tooth Galleries, London: 110. Malkolm Warrington: 11, 16/7, 20/1, 38, 98, 107, 120/1. Whitney Museum of American Art: 36, 86, 116. Copyright: "(c) by A.D.A.G.P. Paris 1979": 7TR, 15, 35, 40, 50, 104, 106, 112, 118. "(c) by S.P.A.D.E.M. Paris 1979": 6, 7L, 28, 41, 42, 43, 52, 57, 58, 62, 81, 92, 97TR, 102.

Introduction

Oil painting has for centuries been the most favoured medium for creative visual expression. One reason for this is simply the ease with which the paint can be used—unlike watercolour, which is normally used in thin applications that dry quickly, oil paint càn be used thickly to provide fascinating textures, or thinly to allow for the build-up of delicate glazes of colour. It dries more slowly too, and a painting can

Below: War was a typical subject of the Renaissance canvas. Shown here is The Battle of San Romano *(c. 1455) by Paolo Uccello.*

2

therefore be worked on over a period of time so that ideas can be developed and the image improved. Another reason for its popularity is that oil paint is more durable. It has a greater resistance to damp than watercolour and can be successfully used on a variety of surfaces from paper to canvas. But above all this, is the paint's immense superiority over other media in terms of colour. You have only to look at the paintings of Rembrandt, the master of muted shadow from which warm earth colours sparkle out in detail, or the work of Monet who

Opposite: Another great theme of classical painting, the birth of Christ. Nativity *by Piero della Francesca (c. 1472).*
One of the most famous of Jan van Eyck's paintings (below), the dignified and moving Marriage of Giovanni Arnolfini *(1434).*
Jan and Hubert van Eyck are the two Flemish painters who are often believed to have 'discovered' oil painting.

The dramatic and violent aspect of nature was frequently explored by Turner. Shown here is Snowstorm-Steamboat off a Harbour's Mouth *c. (1842).*

manipulated oil colour until it captured the iridescence of light as it played upon his surroundings, to realize how very much more versatile and rich the finished work can be.

It is always advisable to understand the background history of any skill before crossing over to a study of its methods and principles. Often this will supply you with an amazing wealth of inspiration as you learn to translate what has been accomplished in the past into your own terms. This is especially true of oil painting.

Throughout the fifteenth and sixteenth centuries the main theme for painting was religion, as it had been for centuries before the advent of the oil medium. The Roman Catholic Church was, after all, the dominant force politically and financially, and it often provided the most obvious patronage for works of art which illustrated its teachings. During (and after) the Renaissance there were also individual private patrons, such as the enlightened Medici family in Florence, whose support of the visual arts encouraged the development of new approaches to subject matter: portraiture, Arcadian themes, historical glorifications of the city state—in Florence and Venice particularly. It was a time of discovery and innovation. Each creative mind was contributing to new concepts both

One of the major artistic movements of eighteenth century France was the Neo-Classic school. Shown here is one of its famous examples The Death of Marat *by David (1793).*

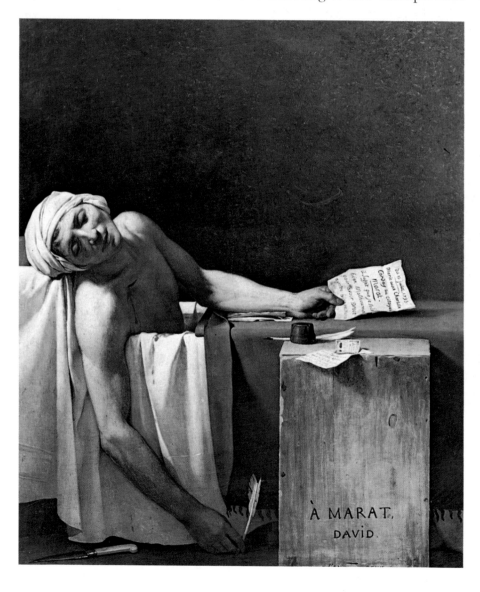

aesthetic and technical: Uccello's overriding obsession was perspective; Botticelli's a poetic, ephemeral world; and Piero della Francesca instilled a quiet humanism into his work.

The opulent wealth of Venice supported the ultimate in glorification with the grandiose paintings of Titian, Tintoretto and Veronese. Many of the works of these men, although technically of religious subjects, became vehicles for individual artistic vision, and the original theme became subservient to it. By the sixteenth and seventeenth centuries, Claude and Poussin were still painting idyllic landscapes and figure composition based on allegorical themes, but the gradual evolutionary process had begun, and subject matter and the approach to painting were changing.

The Impressionists completely transformed the subject matter of painting, firmly removing it from the studio to the open air. Renoir's Luncheon of the Boating Party *(1881) typically captures an ordinary daily event.*

The stability of the southern church continued, but the authority of the Roman Catholic Church was seriously questioned in Northern Europe, then swept aside by the Reformation. The Dutch, having gained religious, and with it political independence from the Spanish, proceeded to establish powerful mercantile trading links across the known world. With success came the rise of a wealthy merchant class which, in its turn, created a new patronage for different types of works of art: seascapes, townscapes, interiors, landscapes and portraits. Accurate, realistic on a domestic scale, these paintings were not just works of art but records of the life-style and attributes of the rich middle class of the time. Genre painting, as it became known, gives a vivid record of the life-style of the wealthy in seventeenth-century Holland.

The twentieth century continued the revolution in painting begun by the Impressionists. Above: The Burning Giraffe *by Salvador Dali (1935) and Left:* Composition in Red, Yellow and Blue *by Mondrian (c. 1940) show how diverse the styles of modern painting can be.*

A detail of an Abstract Expressionist work titled Convergence *by Jackson Pollock (1952).*

By the eighteenth and nineteenth centuries the activity of painting was also changing. Whereas before even landscapes had been firmly anchored in the studio, now there was a change. In England, for example, there were Turner's and Constable's powerful landscapes; one so dramatically capturing the violence of natural phenomena, the other casting a sensitive and affectionate eye on the wind, rain and sunlight filtering onto his Suffolk landscape. They were important not only because they were producing major works of art but also because, although the projects were still being completed in the studio, both artists went outdoors, to the subject, for the first important sketches. In Spain political themes were added to the range of subject matter when Goya's vicious loathing of misused power in which the common people were pawns, was translated into visual terms. It was in France however, where artistic factions were torn between the Neo-Classicism of David and the highly emotional Romantic work of Delacroix and Gericault, that the next major step was made, the repercussions of which are still felt to this day. A small group of artists—Rousseau, Millet and Corot—were the major figures. Settled around Barbizon, they began painting directly from nature, recording the everyday scenes of life— the fields attended by labourers, humble village life and the landscape itself—a theme which was further subscribed to and glorified by Courbet. The seeds of change began to grow furiously. The Impressionists pursued the issue of open-air painting and enlarged even further upon subject matter. Landscape remained the core of interest to all except

Degas; but new, seemingly outrageous, subjects became a basis upon which to build their overriding obsession with light—rail stations, street scenes, women at their toilet, café scenes—nothing was taboo. With Lautrec came even more startling works, with his rapid studies in oil of brothels and prostitutes.

The criteria that had imposed standards of approach and translation of subject within fairly strict confines were finally swept away, leaving the way clear for the successive artistic revolutions of the twentieth century. Picasso, Braque, Léger, Matisse, the Dadaists and Surrealists are well known for their innovations in subject matter, traditional dimensional space, colour, and so on, and the strides made then have been sustained through the Abstract Expressionist work of artists such as Jackson Pollock, Franc Kline, and Mark Rothko. The reaction which followed this last movement produced what is called Post-Painterly Abstraction; Kenneth Noland is a prime example. Pop Art, with experimenters like Claes Oldenburg, Andy Warhol, David Hockney and Alan Jones dominated the early sixties. Today realism is back in favour; but it takes on an infinite number of dimensions, which range from the work of the American Photo Realists, Chuck Close, Donald Eddy and Tom Wesselmann, who seem literally to copy photographs, to the quiet interiors, still life studies and figures of William Bailey.

The history of painting has been one of continual experimentation and innovation. Genuine creativity has been left to a relatively few artists who, in expressing their ideas, have extended the oil painting medium by developing techniques that allow the artist's intentions to flourish without making him a slave to those techniques.

Style often develops by reaction—here against Abstract Expressionism—and finds a new identity, (Post-Painterly Abstraction). Apart by Kenneth Noland (1965).
The sixties was the era of Pop Art. Here Whaam! *(1963) an acrylic work by Roy Lichtenstein takes its inspiration from pulp comics, and is an excellent example of Pop Art style.*

Airstream by Ralph Goings (1970) is a superb example of the Photo-Realist technique, which quite literally seems to imitate photographs.

Although it is impossible, and indeed wrong, to say that you should paint in a certain style, it is important to realize that progress can only be made by working on paintings where an end intention or purpose exists. The desire to present your ideas visually is the root from which will grow your skill in using your painting materials to portray that intention. Thus, ideas and techniques progress side by side.

Ideas develop from continual observation of the richness of the colour, form and texture of the visual world. No individual lives in a vacuum; everyone is influenced to some degree by the things around them. As your perception develops, ideas for paintings will emerge. The technical aspects and physical limitations of the medium will, of course, influence how you choose to present such ideas. It is not so much that there are rules you 'must' follow, rather that it is necessary to understand the correct way to use your materials, and the principles of colour and design, in order to execute your ideas properly. Discovering the potential in yourself through a confident use of the medium is what painting is all about. As with any skill there are certain rules—hence the term 'artistic discipline'—but beyond a certain point your sensibilities, allied to your imagination, will become the guiding factor to progress.

Try not to rely upon technical tricks. Each new work should be a fresh challenge. That is not to say that what has been learned from previous attempts should be ignored, but try to avoid such habits as feeling that you know what the result will be before you start, that you have acquired a fixed way of doing something. Remember that each new idea is unique and presents a fresh challenge. This way you control the medium, rather than it controlling you.

Materials

What do you paint with? This might seem a naive question, but there are literally dozens upon dozens of different brushes, an ever expanding colour spectrum of oil paint and a wide range of surfaces upon which to paint. Many of the brushes have specific uses, and each of the surfaces has a very particular quality—some are smooth, some slightly textured, others heavily textured.

A good artists' supplier is an Aladdin's cave of beautiful and expensive things, and deciding what to purchase can be difficult. For the beginner a little money wisely spent will provide sufficient equipment to work with when developing painting skills; as confidence grows, and with it more particular needs, the equipment can be augmented.

Brushes

Brushes have been developed over several hundred years and each one has been designed for a very specific purpose. For instance, it is unwise

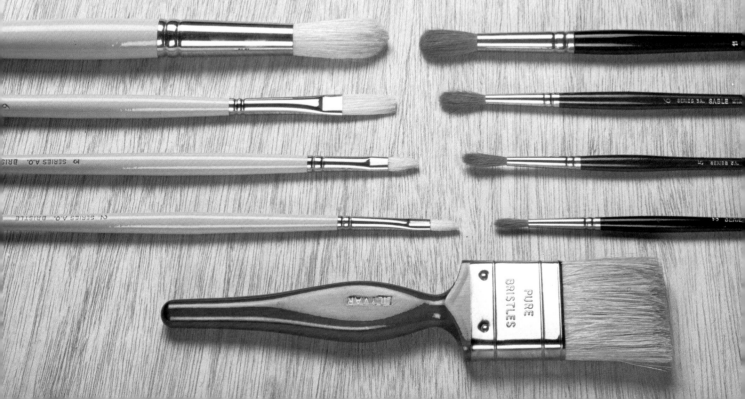

to use a delicate sable hair brush to lay in a large area of colour on a canvas surface. It could be done, but in the process the brush would probably be ruined. The hogs' bristle brush is the work horse. Its stiff bristles are ideal for the transfer of oil paint to canvas as it holds the paint well and makes a crisp fresh mark when applied to the canvas or board.

Sable hair does not have the physical stamina to act as a work horse. Thin, pointed sable hair brushes are for fine detail work and a large flat sable or ox-hair brush is essential for applying thin glazes of colour. It is important to state that although good brushes are expensive—particularly sables—they are worth the investment, for if they are maintained properly they will not only last longer but will retain their

A detail of Mountain of St. Victoire and the Dark Chateau *by Cézanne. The brushwork is an excellent example of block technique.*

Gainsborough's fine sable brushwork is beautifully shown in his painting Mr and Mrs Andrews *(left) while Van Gogh's typical use of thickly applied paint results in complete contrast in style. Below is shown a detail of* The Fields of Arles.

shape better than the less expensive types. Once a brush loses its shape, when loaded with paint it will not respond in the specific way it is meant to.

Although a hogs' bristle brush is tough even it can be ruined, so avoid 'scrubbing' paint onto the canvas surface. Be sure the brush has a sufficient paint load otherwise it will soon cease to be of any use.

At the beginning it is wise to purchase just a few bristle brushes: basically, to begin with, you will need an equal number of round and flat brushes, and large and small ones. One of each no. 2 or 3, no. 6, and no. 10 will give you all you require. As your ability develops you can explore other brush sizes and types, finding ones that might be really useful to you. Augment the basic selection with one or two 2.5cm (1in) and 5cm (2in) decorating brushes. They are used for laying in large areas of oil paint and of course are needed for priming the canvas before you actually start on the work itself.

Brushes made of sable, ox-hair and squirrel are much more delicate and are used for fine work such as detail and glazing. The fine elegant tips of these brushes are extremely sensitive to the amount of pressure applied when putting the brush to the canvas. They should be used with thinned oil paint or small amounts of pure paint.

Good sable hair brushes, the finest being kolinsky, are extremely expensive, and the finest are hand-made. For the professional such brushes may be necessary, but for the novice one small no. 2 or 3 and a medium no. 5 or 6 should be more than adequate and should not be excessive in terms of cost. If larger soft hair brushes are required, an ox-hair or squirrel is the best choice, although they are not of the same quality and are less durable than sable hair.

In recent years, because of the scarcity and increased cost of sable, a number of brush manufacturers have been exploring the use of synthetic fibres for brushes, mainly nylon and polyester.

Initially, because of the poor design of the fibre shape, the brushes would not hold or carry the paint well. But recent improvements have solved this particular problem, and a wide range of synthetic brushes is now manufactured both for oil and watercolour painting. They are relatively cheap and very hard wearing, though they do vary greatly in quality and are really no substitute for natural hair brushes.

Brush maintenance

Brushes, if taken care of properly, will last for many years and still retain their particular characteristics.

Avoid using brushes for mixing large amounts of paint; this is the purpose of a palette knife, although for small amounts the brush is the sensible tool.

When you have finished work for the day, rinse the brushes in a jar of white spirit to release the bulk of paint trapped in the ferrule (the metal ring joining the bristles to the brush handle). Pure turpentine will do the same task but it is more expensive and should be used only to thin oil paint when painting. Blot the brushes by drawing the bristles back and forth on a piece of rag. Then, with white soap and warm water, work up a rich soapy lather in the palm of your hand and gently press the brush into the lather. Do this several times, renewing the lather until all the paint is removed. Rinse the brush in clean water, shake off surplus moisture and press into shape between finger and thumb. Stand the brushes vertically in a jar with the bristles uppermost and leave them to dry. Do not cram the brushes into the container; allow them plenty of space and they will be less likely to become damaged. The brushes can be left in the container until the next time they are required.

Storage

All too often brushes are thrown into boxes, thrust into bags and left without any sort of protection until they are to be used again. Sable and ox-hair brushes are by their very nature particularly prone to damage if treated this way. If the point is damaged or the shape lost, the brush is ruined and will never again be able to do the job for which it was originally designed, so it is important that some form of protection be devised. This can be done easily by making a small tube of stiff paper that will fit around the head of the brush and slightly overlap the handle. For hogs' bristle brushes make a cardboard cylinder blocked at one end to provide protection. There are ready-made containers for brushes on the market but it is less expensive to make your own.

Palette and painting knives
The brush is, of course, the basic tool for paint application, but it is by no means the only one. The knife is a relatively inexpensive tool and very useful. Two basic types of knife exist for the painter: the palette knife, specifically designed for scraping the palette or canvas and for mixing paint, and the painting knife which has a fine springy neck and blade with the sensitivity of touch characteristic of brushes. It is used solely for applying paint to canvas. Painting knives come in a variety of blade sizes, from very large to very small for really delicate, fine application, allowing you literally to draw with the knife.

Below: The Boat *by Nicolas de Staël (1954). This artist is well-known for his work with the palette knife.*

Paints

The colour charts available in art supply stores will give you an idea of the immense range of colours available. To try and make a selection without knowledge or advice is impossible and to consider purchasing all the colours available is an unnecessary expense.

Oil paints are divided into two groups, determined by the nature of the pigment: organic colours, those whose colouring agent is found in nature, and mineral (inorganic) colours, pigments derived from the soil and chemical processes. Mineral colours have greatly extended the range of colours available and they are more permanent (fade less quickly) than the organic colours—a useful attribute for good craftsmen who wish their work to maintain its true colour. Check the manufacturer's colour chart which should indicate the permanence of the paints as established by them.

Oil paints are available in two qualities—student and artist: for the beginner, student oil colours should be purchased. Although their quality is not as refined as artist oil colours, they will allow you to become accustomed to the texture and the mixing and thinning possibilities of the paint at substantially less cost. The following colours are recommended for a student palette: Ivory black, Titanium white, Cadmium yellow, Cadmium lemon, Cadmium red, Alizarin crimson, Ultramarine blue, Cobalt blue, Winsor violet, Viridian. These will supply the basic colour requirements, and from them you will be able to mix any additional colours you will need. (The chapter Handling Colour explains the advantages of these as basic colours to begin working with.) As confidence and ability grow, and with it an understanding of the medium, it would be practical to begin using artist colours. Their colour is richer and more vibrant and the paint covers the canvas really well.

Different colours dry at different rates due to differences in their chemical make-up: some are slow, some are moderately fast, some very fast. The drying time is further altered by the mediums you may be using and thickness with which the colour is applied. Most paint manufacturers should be able to supply you with a list of drying times. This obviously influences the results and the way you work: you may want to scrape away a very dark colour to substitute a lighter one, only to find the darker colour dried and immovable.

Mediums

A medium is used to thicken or thin the paint, making the colour richer or else extending the pigment to allow thin glazes of colour to be laid over one another. The key medium is spirit of turpentine (turps). It is mostly used for thinning the paint and thus is obviously useful when

mixing colours. Always purchase turpentine from an art supply store as you are then assured that the quality is pure and will in no way discolour the pigment.

Linseed oil is the most useful additive if you want to try glazing or thick impastos of paint as it gives the paint the necessary flexibility for these techniques. Disadvantages of linseed oil are that it slows down the drying process, can yellow the paint and can also lead to cracking and wrinkling of the paint surface. A very refined linseed oil (stand oil) is less likely to lead to these problems, so check the grade of the oil before purchasing.

Varnishes

Varnishes are resins dissolved in oil or spirits, and are fast drying. They are used primarily for providing a coating or protective skin over the finished work. They are also used by some artists when mixing colours to help speed drying. The most commonly used is retouching varnish.

One of the great advantages of oil over other paints is the barely noticeable change in colour from the wet state to the dry. What does happen, though, is a dulling or deadening of the colour, and if nothing is done to counter this you will find that as each day of painting passes, you will be inclined to use duller and duller colours to adjust to the colour already drying on the canvas. Therefore, before resuming work on the canvas, take a large, really clean brush (no. 10 flat squirrel is ideal), load it with retouching varnish and paint the areas that have deadened during drying. As soon as the varnish is applied, the original

Au Salon de la Rue des Moulins *by Toulouse Lautrec shows thinly applied layers of colour with some of the original sketch work showing through.*

freshness of the colour will reappear, allowing for really accurate colour matching. Fresh paint can then be applied over the retouching varnish without any technically detrimental side effects. For the same purpose, retouching varnish can be used in small quantities as an additive to the paint.

If you are using retouching varnish as a protective coating on a finished painting, apply the varnish quickly once or twice when the painting is thoroughly dry—six months is usually an adequate drying time. Avoid disturbing the surface too much or the colours could be dislodged. Always remember to store the painting carefully while the varnish dries to avoid dust settling on the sticky surface. Alternatively, you may choose to use clear picture varnish as a final protection, although this results in a high gloss surface that interferes with viewing the work. Clear picture varnish is actually retouching varnish in a more concentrated form. The great advantage with modern varnishes is the unlikelihood of any darkening with age—a problem that so besets the Old Masters. The varnish can usually be purchased in several sizes for economy and is also available in aerosol containers which give splendid control during application. When using either, be sure that the painting and the work area are free of dust.

Although many other types of mediums and varnishes exist these will provide all that is required for the beginner; many professionals use no more.

As mentioned earlier, paint drying times vary and just how much time you have available in any one day, week or month to set aside for drying will influence your work. For the beginner a regular period set aside several times a week to allow the paint to dry is necessary if any progress is to be made. Without help, many colours dry very slowly, but there are now special oils available which can be added to the paint to speed up the drying process. Particularly useful are strong drying oils no. 1 and no. 2, poppy oil drying and linseed oil drying.

Strong drying oil no. 1 consists of boiled linseed oil and lead driers, and should be thinned with pure turpentine. The only unsatisfactory thing about it is that it tends to darken the colour.

Strong drying oil no. 2 consists of boiled linseed oil and cobalt driers. Like oil no. 1, it will increase the drying rate at some expense to the colour's brightness. Its advantage is that it is paler and more fluid, making it easier to mix with the paint. If thinning use pure turpentine. Poppy oil drying is a mixture of refined poppy oil and cobalt driers and is extremely useful for accelerating the drying time of white and pale colours.

Linseed oil drying is a combination of raw linseed oil and manganese driers. It is probably the most satisfactory of the four listed as it has little influence on the oil colour.

Palettes

The traditional view of the artist holding an oval-shaped palette is somewhat misleading. That is not to say it is not used—it certainly is. The great advantage of all hand-held palettes is the close proximity of the mixing surface to the canvas, which really does aid judgement in mixing accurate colour. There are literally dozens of shapes and sizes available: some are large and best for studio work; others are small, rectangular and ideal for putting into a shopping bag for outside work.

When purchasing a hand-held palette try it for balance. If it seems uncomfortable it can lead to considerable annoyance when working. With this form of palette it is convenient to use dippers as containers for turps and other mediums. Dippers are small cups available in several sizes as singles or doubles and simply slip onto the edge of the palette.

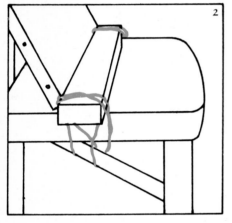

Support for an outdoors easel is often necessary.
Fig. 1 Here the easel is bound to pegs in the ground.
Fig. 2 An impromptu easel can be made from an old kitchen chair with a bar of wood tied across the seat as a support for the canvas.

Because of the natural size restriction of a hand-held palette the actual mixing area is quite small and, for large-scale work, or for working exclusively indoors, you will find an old tabletop provides a more substantial area. Also a tabletop serves as a shelf for brushes and other materials not actually in use but readily available should they be required. Even if using the hand-held palette it is useful to have a small table close by on which to lay your equipment and supplement your mixing space.

Easels

This is the single most expensive piece of equipment you will require. As with the other materials, several types exist, from the light compact sketching easel to the large studio ratchet type. The most sensible easel, as it provides excellent stability in the studio and is convenient for out-side work, is the sketch box type. This easel folds into a compact box that has a carrying handle and provides storage for paints and other equipment.

Outdoors in any sort of breeze, a lightweight easel with a canvas attached is likely to blow over. To counter this problem, carry some sharp pointed pegs of wood and some nylon cord plus a small hammer. Having placed the easel in position, tap the pegs into the soil parallel to the leg positions and bind the tops of the pegs to the legs (fig. 1). This will provide a fairly rigid support for the easel.

A short-term alternative, but useful only for indoor work, is an old kitchen chair with a bar of wood tied across the seat. The canvas is propped between the bar of wood and the back of the chair (fig. 2).

Canvas

The finest canvas support is linen. It is certainly the strongest fabric for oil painting and has the best textural quality, but cotton duck is extremely popular and reliable and is far cheaper. The very best canvas has few faults in it. To check the quality hold it up to the light—the closer the weave and the fewer the joins the better. Ready-primed canvases can be obtained from good art supply stores and although without doubt they can be excellent in quality they are also extremely expensive. Ready-stretched canvases are available in a wide range of sizes and quality should the idea of stretching your own be daunting or too much trouble. However, purchasing your own unprimed canvas to be stretched at home is the most satisfactory solution both from aesthetic and cost points of view: it is cheaper and you have complete control regarding the size and quality.

Stretching canvas

The wooden framework over which the canvas is stretched is called a stretcher. Ready-made ones are available in varying lengths and the best have machine-made mitred corners which slot together for easy assembly. A less expensive alternative is to make your own stretcher frame.

Using ready-made stretchers
First fit the stretcher pieces together using a set square to ensure that the corners form right angles. Lay the canvas on a flat surface, smoothing

In his work Jealousy *Munch has applied paint very thinly, allowing the texture of the canvas to show through.*

out wrinkles, and put the stretcher onto the canvas, placing it squarely on the weave of the canvas. Do not worry about folds and creases in the canvas due to storage; they will disappear once the canvas is sized. Cut the canvas leaving a 5cm (2in) margin all around the stretcher (fig. 3).

Make sure you have the stretcher the correct way around. The front facing surface (the side which is laid face down on the canvas) will have rounded and bevelled edges so that the actual face of the stretcher slopes away slightly from the canvas (fig. 4). This prevents a ridge from forming on the stretched canvas.

To attach the canvas to the stretcher, use either 6mm ($\frac{1}{2}$in) upholstery tacks or a staple gun—the latter is certainly easier, as one hand can be used to stretch the canvas on the frame while the other fires the gun.

Canvas must be stretched before it can be used.
Fig. 3 A 5cm (2in) margin is left all around the stretcher when cutting the canvas.
Fig. 4 The face of the stretcher slopes away slightly from the canvas.

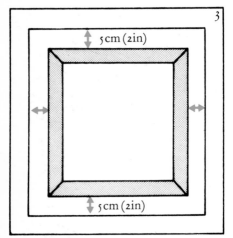

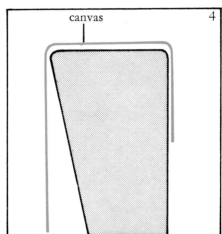

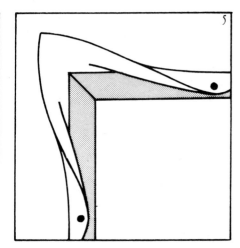

Fig. 5 The canvas is attached at the centre of each stretcher piece.
Fig. 6 Sequence of working.
Fig. 7 Mitre the fabric at the corners. Tack or staple, making sure that mitre fold aligns with corner of the stretcher.
Fig. 8 When stretching a canvas over 1.5m (5ft) square, use canvas pliers to grip and pull fabric.
Fig. 9 A mitre box

However it is a fairly expensive investment for a beginner to make so, by all means stick to tacks if you prefer.

Having checked that the bevelled edge is face down and that the warp and weft are aligned at right angles with the stretcher, all is ready to begin. Fold one edge of the canvas over the stretcher piece and tack or staple in the centre to the uppermost edge. Repeat this operation with the opposite side, then the two other sides, pulling the canvas evenly over the stretcher. The canvas is thus attached at the centre of each stretcher piece (fig. 5). Working from each centre point, either side of the tack or staple and from side to opposite side, carry on pulling the canvas evenly across the stretcher, tacking or stapling every 5cm (2in) to within 5cm (2in) at each end. Fig. 6 shows the order in which to work. Mitre the fabric at the corners by neatly folding one side under the other (fig. 7). Tack or staple securely, being sure that the fold of the mitre aligns with the corner of the canvas stretcher. The canvas should be taut but not excessively so since when the size is applied it will shrink. Stretching a canvas in excess of 1.5m (5ft) square will prove awkward without the help of canvas pliers (fig. 8). These are used to grip the canvas, pull it over the stretcher, and hold it in place while tacking.

Making a stretcher frame

The equipment necessary for the construction of home-made stretchers should be available in the average household except possibly the clamp used in conjunction with a grooved mitre box (fig.9). This is used to cut mitre joints and holds corners while glueing. It is also used for framing. Other necessary tools are: tenon saw, screwdriver, tapping hammer, drill and bit, countersink bit, ruler, pencil, screws, panel pins [picture nails] and wood glue. Prepared 5cm x 2.5cm (2in x 1in) wood is an ideal dimension to use for average-size stretches from 51cm x 76cm (20in x 30in) and will be adequate up to 1.5m (5ft) square as long as a reinforcing bar is added across the middle.

Decide upon the dimensions of your stretcher and mark the lengths on the wood. Place the wood in the clamp and saw the angles along the length as shown in fig. 10. Then glue and screw each corner together. Alternatively, use corrugated corner fasteners (fig. 11).

To lift the canvas away from the stretcher attach a ridge of beading with glue and panel pins [picture nails] (fig. 12).

Large stretchers can be constructed in the same way with the addition of a central reinforcing bar, but due to the extra tension, it is wise to reinforce the corners either with an L-shaped metal angle plate or some triangles of hardboard glued and nailed to the back of the stretcher at each corner (fig. 13). Stretch the canvas as described.

Linen canvas, though tough, is very susceptible to atmospheric changes and should always be used on wedgable stretchers. A real disadvantage of home-made stretchers is that they cannot be wedged and cannot re-tension the canvas should it become slack.

Wedging

Manufactured stretchers have a distinct advantage over home-made types as they incorporate in the cut joint a small slot into which a triangular wooden wedge can be tapped. This allows the canvas to be re-tensioned should it become slack during the application of paint. Building up paint areas with a knife or scraping away paint are both likely to cause slackening.

Do not wedge after stretching as any slackness in the raw canvas will be taken up with the sizing. When wedging is required place two wedges per corner and tap them in gently until the canvas is re-tensioned. On large canvases with a full cross bar, you will find additional slots cut where the bar joins the stretcher piece. Wedges are usually supplied with the stretchers. All that wedging does is to open the corner joints slightly.

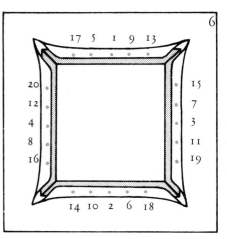

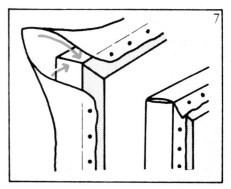

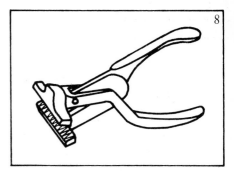

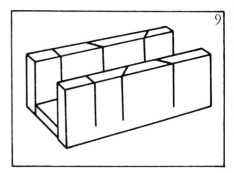

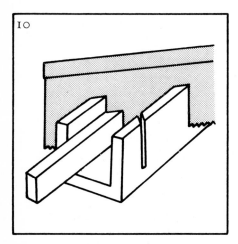

Board

Man-made boards, particularly hardboard, provide an excellent and resilient base for oil painting. Hardboard, if of relatively small dimensions, is sufficiently rigid not to need battening supports, but once above 51cm x 41cm (20in x 16in) it has a natural pliability and will require reinforcement. To do this, construct a frame of 5cm x 2.5cm (2in x 1in) wood as you did for the canvas ground. Smear the facing surface of the frame with wood adhesive and lay the hardboard onto the frame. Use 2cm (½in) countersink panel pins [picture nails] at 5cm (2in) intervals along each edge to secure the board to the frame. Wipe away surplus glue.

This same reinforcing procedure applies to any other pliable board, such as plywood. Unfortunately, board surfaces when primed are extremely slippery, unpleasant surfaces on which to paint. To counter

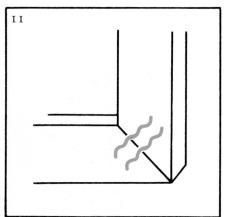 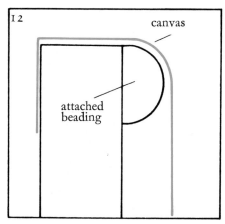 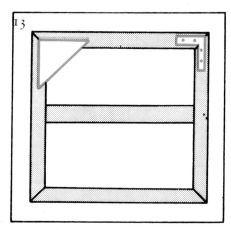

Fig. 10 Sawing the angles of the wood for the stretcher.
Fig. 11 Fitting the corners with corrugated corner fasteners.
Fig. 12 To lift canvas away from stretcher, attach a ridge of beading.
Fig. 13 Large stretchers need their corners reinforced as shown here.

Right: Painters use a wide range of surfaces. The Lady of Shalott by William Holman Hunt is worked in oil on a wood panel.

this problem a toothed (textured) surface can be provided with butter muslin [cheesecloth] sized onto the board. Cut a piece of muslin [cheesecloth] allowing a 5cm (2in) margin all around to fold to the wrong side of the board. Apply size to the board and stretch the muslin [cheesecloth] across it. Smooth out any ridges that occur or they will prove a real nuisance when painting. The size not only provides a sealer but firmly attaches the muslin [cheesecloth] to the board.

Paper

Paper is often used as a painting surface, but it needs to be stretched first and then sealed (priming is optional) before it will provide an ideal surface. Various qualities of paper exist from smooth through to coarse. What you use depends on personal preference, but it must be of good quality if it is to provide a reasonable base. Ordinary drawing paper will not be suitable, particularly at the stretching stage. Stretching is done by soaking the paper in clean water until saturated. Make sure the paper is not creased in any way; this would cause a fault and the paper

27

would rip as it stretches. Carefully remove the paper from the bath allowing water to drain off. Lay the paper on a drawing board making sure the right side of the paper is facing upwards. (In most hand-made papers it is relatively easy to see the right side on which to work, but with some of the good quality manufactured types it is difficult: if scrutinized carefully, the wrong side will be seen to have a fine orderly mesh texture on it.) Gently wipe the paper with a clean dry cloth, eliminating any bubbles as you would when wallpapering, then quickly lay a moistened 5cm (2in) wide gummed paper strip around all four sides overlapping 2cm ($\frac{3}{4}$in) on the paper and 3cm ($1\frac{1}{4}$in) on the board. Leave the board flat as this will allow the paper to dry evenly. If the board is stood on end the paper will dry unevenly because the moisture drains from the top to the bottom, keeping the bottom gum strip wet so that it does not glue firmly to the paper. As the uneven drying continues the bottom edge will separate from the gum strip. If this happens, the stretching process must be repeated. The paper will always cockle during drying, but as long as it is kept flat it will dry into an immaculate smooth surface.

Although it is advisable to size and prime the paper, it is possible to work directly on an unprepared paper. Beware, though, of paint sinking into the paper surface.

If stretching paper is too troublesome and canvas too expensive, there are various manufactured alternatives: canvas boards made of cotton canvas mounted on thick cardboard; oil sketching boards with a canvas graining incorporated into the prime coating; and heavy coarse grained or medium grained paper sketching pads made especially for oil paints.

Sizing

Oil reacts upon canvas causing it to rot, but a canvas should be coated with an oil-based primer before you paint your picture on it. A coating of size, applied directly to the canvas, provides a barrier between it and the primer, so preventing the possible gradual destruction of the canvas. Traditionally, the finest size is rabbit skin glue, purchased in small sheets from art supply stores. If not available ask for the best alternative. It is brittle, so be careful when breaking it into small pieces as it is very sharp.

To prepare the size allow it to soak in water until soft and then heat through slowly until all the solids have dissolved. Do not boil. Allow the mixture to cool and apply to the canvas just before it begins to gel, using a large clean brush. The size must be applied as evenly and smoothly as possible to facilitate easier and even application of the primer. If the size is too hot it will soak directly into the canvas fibres rather than form a film covering to protect the fabric from the oil primer. Make up only a sufficient amount for the canvas you are sizing as the

Although it is mainly regarded as the surface for watercolours, paper is often used by oil artists too. Shown opposite is Woman by a Window *(Degas), a beautiful oil on paper work.*

29

mixture will deteriorate in a very short time, and give off a really foul, penetrating odour. Discard any excess immediately.

When applying the size an immediate shrinkage takes place, tensioning the canvas and removing any odd creases that might have remained after stretching. This is particularly so with linen canvas; cotton canvas should be tensioned more than linen at the stretching stage.

Other commercial sizes are available and will, if used as suggested, prove to be equally as efficient, but perhaps less flexible after application.

Priming the canvas
When the glue size is thoroughly dry proceed to apply a coat of oil-based primer as evenly as possible, using a large decorator's brush. Although two coats should cover most canvases adequately, it very much depends on the coarseness of the canvas you are using and how you are going to apply the oil paint. If you are working with thin paint on coarse canvas a third coat would be useful and provide a smoother surface, otherwise, you could find yourself fighting the texture of the canvas. Make sure each coat is absolutely dry before applying the next, or the prime coat will inevitably crack. With properly prepared canvas there should be no evidence of primer seeping through to the back. If this should happen, it could be one of two things: the size has not been applied correctly or the weave of the canvas is so open that it is impossible for the size to establish a fine skin.

An alternative to oil-based primers is acrylic primer. This is water-based and fast drying—a distinct advantage over oil-based primers. It is not necessary to size canvas or boards before applying this type of primer. There are, however, two problems with acrylic primer: one is that the colour of the oil paint tends to become dull when applied over it (although this can be countered with retouching varnish); the other, though not proven, is the possibility that the oil paint might in time peel off an acrylic primed canvas because of the difference of elasticity.

Gesso is a combination of gypsum and glue size and was used for priming wooden panels and coating surfaces prior to gilding. Today gesso comes in two forms: one is a glue composed of glue size and Titanium white paint which has excellent covering capacity; the other is an acrylic gesso. Both may be used to prime canvas as well as rigid board or panel.

As both gessos are water-based be sure that the surface to be primed is completely oil-free before applying, otherwise they will not adhere to the surface. Glue gesso will prove to be very absorbent to oil paint, so seal the gesso surface with a thin coat of size. This will provide a beautifully smooth surface on which to paint, ideal for highly detailed work.

Handling Colour

The principles involved in using colour do not vary among the visual arts: for oil, as for watercolour, coloured inks, pastels and crayons, the cardinal rule is to experiment first to see how the different colours mix. Only by trial and error will you finally know whether you should put down a layer of one colour first, then a layer of a second colour on top of it, or whether it would be better to mix them together in the palette

A Bigger Splash (*acrylic on canvas*) *by David Hockney uses really pure, brilliant colour to achieve its effect.*

first. Either method can be satisfactory, so work out what's best for you, given the medium and materials you are using. Whenever experiments here call for white, always use a good, opaque white ground. Colour, even cream, in the ground would influence the applied colours.

Selecting colours

The names given to colours and the colours themselves vary considerably from manufacturer to manufacturer—crimson or violet, to name only two examples, can vary remarkably from one range to another. Since individual colours tend to have traces of other colours in them, it is very difficult to find a 'true' red, a 'true' yellow and 'true' blue. Of course, an easy compromise, to take care of any problems, is to choose two versions of each primary colour. Although there are many colours to choose from, some of which are mentioned in this chapter, a basic set of colours could be based on the list which follows:

Cadmium yellow —contains some primary red
Cadmium lemon —contains traces of primary blue
Cadmium red —veers toward primary yellow
Alizarin crimson —contains some primary blue
Cobalt blue —contains a little primary yellow
Ultramarine blue —contains a little primary red
Ivory black —as neutral a black as possible, one that is dense
Titanium white —other whites tend to be either transparent, silvery or bluish white

Because the mixing theory does not work in practice (the impurities interfering again) you cannot achieve a clear purple by mixing; so try, say, Winsor violet. Green can cause similar problems.

Making a colour wheel

A colour wheel explains at a glance how colours relate to one another. Every artist makes one up at some point, and it provides an invaluable method of teaching the mixing of colours. Keep it; you will find it useful.

Prepare a pure white ground. At first use the colours straight from the tube and be particular about using only very clean brushes so that your colours remain pure. First paint an area of Cadmium yellow, then next to it an area of Cadmium lemon. From Cadmium lemon, work around in a circle adding Cobalt (a blue containing yellow) followed by Ultramarine blue, Alizarin crimson followed by Cadmium red. (In other words, first paint the chosen primary colour influenced first by one other primary, then with the other, until you quite literally come full circle.) Try mixing all three of the primary colours together on a palette until you have a neutral grey. You will find it impossible to do this by combining equal amounts of each colour, because some colours are inherently darker or stronger than others; you must gauge the quantities needed by watching the mixtures. When the grey is as neutral as you can get it, paint a patch in the centre of the wheel.

The three *primary* colours are red, yellow and blue. In theory, you should be able to mix all the colours you wish using different proportions of these three primary colours, for they represent all the colours that exist. In practice, however, various chemical properties in the manufacture of different brands of paint do influence the colours when they are mixed together. Again, theoretically, by mixing all primary colours together you should get black; but in practice, because of paint's variable properties, you would be more likely to end up with a darkish grey, a 'non-colour'.

Secondary colours are pure colours mixed from any two primaries. Orange, green and purple are all secondary colours. Experiment with Cadmium yellow and Cadmium red until you get a clear orange, midway between yellow and red. Paint an arc around the outside of the corresponding yellow and red areas of the wheel. Continue the exercise by

Completing the colour wheel (fig. 1). Making a wheel of your own explains very quickly how colours relate to one another.

Alyscamps at Arles by Gauguin shows how an unusual and often non-realistic use of colour can give added life and vitality to the painting.

making a green from Cadmium lemon and Cobalt blue and paint a green arc around the corresponding yellow and blue section. Purple is more difficult to make, but see what you can come up with by mixing Alizarin crimson and Ultramarine blue, then paint in the obligatory arc. (Fig. 1 shows how the colour wheel should appear when finished.)

Each of the secondary colours is a mixture of two primary colours: for instance, purple is a mixture of red and blue. The primary colour not concerned in the making of purple is yellow, and yellow is therefore the *complementary* colour of purple. If you mix any complementary colours together they will go grey or 'non-coloured' because you are, in effect, combining the three primary colours.

From the painted wheel you can spot the complementary pairs. Look at a primary colour area, then look for the arc of colour opposite it on the far side of the circle; this is the complement. Those colours which are called complementaries are genuine opposites. Think of them as colour combinations for clothes. Would you wear red with green, yellow with mauve or purple, blue with orange? You cannot say, as they used to in the past, that 'red with green should not be seen', since the right choice of red with the right green could look stunning. Most likely, because they are opposites, you would think twice about wearing them together. All opposite or complementary colours should therefore be used together both wisely and sparingly. Experimenting with the various components of the colour wheel helps to give some idea of the variety of colours that can be mixed using the suggested palette of primary and secondary colours. These colours probably won't provide all of your colour needs, but as you become more experienced in colour mixing and matching, you can be a better judge of which other colours you might need. Now that you have begun to mix secondary colours, experiment further, using other colours, so that you can have a better idea of what is possible and what is not. For instance, you could experiment with different proportions of colour. Some pigments have tremendous strength and others have only a little (a very little black has an obvious influence on Cadmium lemon and will turn it green).

Any colours other than primaries or secondaries are known as *tertiaries,* that is, mixes of three colours or more. For example, try mixing a purple-grey using black, white and a touch of Winsor violet. If it is not sufficiently purple add Alizarin crimson; because of the yellow tinge, Cadmium red would not really be suitable, for when it is mixed with the black element, the grey would move towards a brown.

Do not hesitate to explore: paint small areas of the experimental mixes onto a sheet of paper, carefully listing all the colours used. Then pin the paper to the wall as a reminder to you when you start painting.

Green will make a red dull, but the right blue may darken the red and leave it fairly pure. A very small quantity of black will darken a colour, but its purity will disappear and it may be changed into another colour entirely. Remember black mixed with yellow will produce a dirty greenish brown, compared to the bright green obtained by mixing Lemon yellow and Cerulean blue.

So colour mixing is a question of degree. As previously stated, either black, green or blue could be used to darken a red, depending on how colourless or 'un-red' you want the result to be. The same holds true for the other primary colours. Blue can be darkened by a little red, black or orange; black will possibly kill its purity (less so if it is Ultramarine, more so if it is Cerulean); orange will neutralize it, making it greyer or browner according to the amount used; a hint of red will keep it basically blue, but will turn it purple or mauve if used too freely. Yellow can be darkened by a little red, black or mauve, but it will be

Above: Nu à Contre Jour *by Pierre Bonnard. The nude is a subtle surface on which light falls in fascinating ways. Here the artist is exploring the shades of colour influenced by the source of light, both on the model's skin and on the room itself.*

Above: Ice *by Richard Lindner.*
The painting shows an effective
use of primary colours.

quickly tainted and will soon lose its 'yellowness'. Red may deepen it before turning it orange; black, we have already seen, will turn it into a dull green; and mauve will neutralize it by pushing it towards grey or brown.

So brown can be made by mixing complementaries together, being arrived at before grey by varying quantities slightly. Red mixed with black will also produce brown.

Sometimes a mixed colour (especially brown or green) will be more satisfactory than one straight from a tube.

Darken a brown by using blue, especially Ultramarine. This gives a much richer, deeper colour than by adding black.

To darken secondary colours (orange, mauve and green) without making them dull, add their darkest natural ingredient: red for orange, blue for mauve or green. A crimson added to an orange which was made with Cadmium red will alter it subtly, making it less 'fiery'. A similar thing will happen to a mauve when Ultramarine or Monestial blue are added instead of the original Cobalt or Cerulean. White, of course, will lighten a colour, but so will yellow if it is added to orange, red or green.

Remember that when using any paints, not just oils, the more colours you mix together, the duller or greyer the result. This is why a professional artist will use artist oils or watercolours: they have more colour pigment in them and can therefore be mixed further before dulling occurs. For this reason it is impossible to get a bright mauve or turquoise from lesser-quality paints, but fairly easy to do with artist oil colours.

Indeed, when you do mix a grey in artist oil colours, you will find that it is possible to achieve coloured greys which are much, much more interesting than grey made by mixing black and white alone; a whole picture could be built around them. Sometimes a mauve-grey or greenish grey, for example, is more satisfying to look at, and is richer, than a straightforward mauve or green. If you place such a colour next to its opposite, in this case against yellow or red respectively, you will see an optical vibration occur that may even be quite disturbing to the eye (see the experiment with cut-out colours in this chapter).

Indeed, there are two major ways to achieve this vibration or glow with colour. Both are visually dangerous tools, but ones which produce spectacular results when successful.

One is called the law of 'simultaneous contrast'. If you were painting a sun and you placed a cold Lemon yellow next to a warmer Chrome yellow, both being surrounded by shades of cream and Naples yellow of similar tone, the result would be a radiant glow of colour. If there were small, pure white gaps between the colours, and if all the colours were exactly the same light tone, the glow would be increased enormously. Imagine a whole painting done this way.

Similarly, two opposite or complementary colours placed next to each other will produce a different kind of vibration or 'flicker' because of their different optical wavelengths. At extremes, it is difficult to focus a red next to a green, hence the flicker. This can also be demonstrated using black and white, as in fig. 2 by Bridget Riley. Here the lines are so cleverly controlled that we cannot focus on them (try counting them!). The strong difference between black and white short-circuits the eye, and pairs of opposite colours can be produced by staring at the picture

closely; move it very slightly to create a wave-effect. Such paintings, some of which are 6m (20ft) across, can actually induce a violent feeling of sickness.

So, by placing, say, simultaneously contrasting yellows next to various shades of their complementaries (light mauve), we can produce a glow which is stronger and certainly richer than any effect achieved with fluorescent colours.

Remember that some pure colours are naturally stronger than others. A very rich colour, and therefore one which can only seldom be used pure, is Geranium Lake. Put your brightest colours on first, then put pure Geranium Lake onto your picture, and the others will pale into insignificance. But mix it with a mauve or purple and where they were previously dull they will take on a new lease of life.

Crest by Bridget Riley (acrylic) fig. 2 demonstrates the flickering effect produced by two opposite colours, in this case black and white, when used next to one another.

The act of painting reduced to its simplest terms is about colour. It is now time, therefore, to consider the effects and the optical influence of one colour against another. Primaries are relatively stable and are not much influenced by other colours; neither are secondaries. Tertiaries, however, can be influenced very much indeed—in fact, their appearance can be radically altered by the nature of surrounding colour, a phenomenon which is sometimes referred to as induced colour. The exercise illustrated by fig. 3 demonstrates how colours can change one another. In order to achieve the desired effect of this exercise, equal proportions and complete cleanliness of colour are mandatory, so it is wise to adopt the painting and cutting-out method in order to avoid any smudging of colour or rough edges which could affect the results.

Take seven average-sized sheets of drawing paper and paint one a middle blue-grey and one each black, green, blue, yellow, red and purple. Make sure the colour is as opaque as possible but not too thick or it will take a long time to dry. When the paint is dry, divide the blue-grey sheet into 2.5cm (1in) squares and cut out the squares with a craft knife or scissors. Cut a 10cm (4in) square from each of the coloured sheets, then arrange the large squares on a sheet of white cardboard or paper, leaving about a 4cm (1½in) gap between each one. Finally, attach a small blue-grey square to the centre of each large coloured square. The results will be quite surprising for each of the small blue-grey squares will appear to be different hues of that colour. You can experiment in this way, *ad infinitum*, using, for instance a primary or secondary colour for the central square. Even in the case of primaries, apparent visual change will certainly occur though it will not be as pronounced as with a tertiary.

In the case of primary colours, the amount used in relation to another colour determines the extent to which the primary will be influenced. For although they are stable, if they are used only in small proportions they can be influenced—a fact which is true for most colours. Fig. 4 used Cadmium red as the primary and two sizes of centre square, leaving A and C with a very narrow border and B and D surrounded by a heavy border. In squares A and C the borders have no obvious optical influence over the red, so they remain identical. But in squares B and D the two border colours induce a colour change on the red.

From these experiments you can gather how colours can influence one another. By now, having observed colour and shape as they occur within your natural environment, the terrors attached to using (or misusing) colour should evaporate, and it will become easier to make colours work for you so that you can achieve the effects you wish to create.

Fig. 4 Although a primary colour such as cadmium red is usually very stable, and not easily influenced by other colours, as these sample squares show, if used in small proportions, the primary can be affected (in squares B and D).

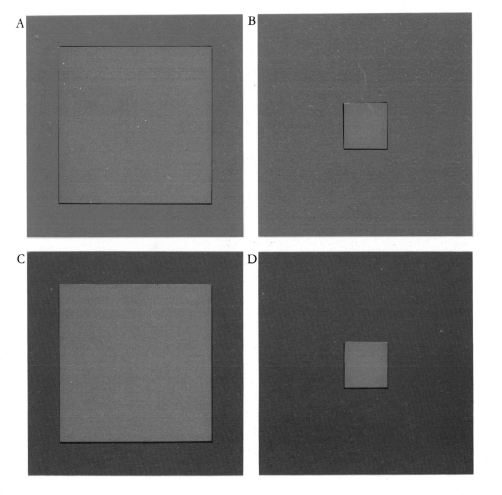

Fig. 5 Nu Dans le Bain *by Pierre Bonnard explores the most challenging surfaces for the painter —water and human flesh.*
Fig. 6 Monet's Rouen Cathedral, West Facade *is one of several studies of the same subject, constantly seeking the changing facets of light and colour throughout the day and into the early evening.*

Colour at work

Colour has symbolic value in every society and has had since the beginning of history. Black in many cultures, for instance, is worn to indicate death and mourning. Twentieth-century industrial culture has developed its own colour symbols within its transport system; red for stop, green for go are obvious examples; many others exist. There is an established order of colour within the universe too: the sky is generally blue, the grass nearly always green, a grape either green or black, and so on. Such colours found in nature are called *local colours*, that is the colour of the natural object as it actually is, without being altered or influenced by light or shadow. Obviously, however, such objects can and are influenced—by natural as well as artificial sources of light—and these forms can produce a profound alteration on the appearance. It is always important to remember the influence of light when painting. The landscape in the distance seemingly becomes bluish-grey in colour because distance and atmosphere diffuse the local colour. The most obvious influence of daylight or artificial light can be seen on the surface of water. Water literally mirrors the colour above it or around its perimeter. Another highly receptive surface is human flesh. Added to the complex and fascinating contrasts inherent in the human anatomy, it is what makes painting the nude one of the most challenging—and somewhat exasperating—problems the artist has to deal with. The Bonnard painting (fig. 5) of a figure partly submerged in a bath tackles both of these problems. Not only was he trying to capture the effects of light on the water surface but also on the partially submerged figure.

The influence of daylight on the shiny surface of an orange is less evident, as orange is a powerful local colour. But on close viewing, it is possible to notice a colour change if you move the orange from a brightly lit surface into an area of shadow—a blue light (remember blue is the complement of orange) will appear on the shaded areas of the orange, thus altering the appearance of the local colour. On a matt (dull) surface, the influence would appear to be more subtle because the surface is not very reflective.

Fig. 7 Another beautiful example of Monet's skill with light and colour is shown in his work Water Lilies.

Although several nineteenth-century artists, Delacroix, Turner and Constable to name three prime examples, explored the influence of light on colour in the environment, it was only with the advent of the Impressionists that the essentially Renaissance influence on colour perception was modified and changed. Traditionally, light had been used solely as a means of seeing what was being painted, now, with the Impressionists, it was being used deliberately, and as part of the composition, to suggest how it revealed and affected the colour of the subjects being painted. For a short time the Impressionists directed their

Fig. 8 Theories on the subject of colour also fascinated the Neo-Impressionists. Paul Signac's painting The Rotterdam Harbour *(1907) is painted in dots of pure colour, a technique often called pointillism.*

43

energies toward exploring the influence of light on both environment and colour. It was Monet who pursued the issue in the most single-minded way. The studies he did of *Rouen Cathedral* (fig. 6) and *Water Lilies* (fig. 7) are among the most obvious examples of paintings influenced by this line of thought.

On the other hand, the Neo-Impressionists (Seurat, Signac and Cross) developed an elaborate theory of colour, constructing their pictures using dots of pure colour. Fig. 8 shows a painting by Signac demonstrating this colour-mixing technique. This same technique is used in modern half-tone reproduction printing.

Although the Impressionists still influence the visual scene, there are no longer any absolute rules about how colour should be used; it can now be used in any way the artist wishes to use it, to expand and explain his interpretation of his visual world. From the muted richness of a Flemish master to the shimmering dot constructions of Seurat, to the strong simple areas of inter-relating colour used by painters such as Ellsworth Kelly (fig. 9), you can see that colour can be used both to portray the subtleties of the subject being painted, or, indeed, it can itself become the subject of the painting.

Fig. 9 Blue, Black and Red *by Ellsworth Kelly is an effective use of primary colours in strong, simple masses.*

Project: A Still Life

Now that you have tried out the paints and brushes in the exercises given in the previous chapters, you will want to put your knowledge to some practical use. The sooner you begin to paint in earnest, the better.

People paint because they are stimulated by what they see and want to give expression to their feelings in a visual way. Subject sources can be

divided into three basic groups: landscape and townscape, the figure (groups, portraits and self-portraits), and still life.

The still life group is not necessarily an easier subject to paint than landscape or figure composition, but it does present very definite advantages for the beginner that should be considered seriously. First, you have the opportunity to select objects that you personally like. Painting the luxuriant colours in fruit, vegetables and fabrics has long been a favourite challenge and traditional subject source for the artist, from the seventeenth century through to contemporary artists. Simple utensils like a jug, plate and vase, or a mixture of natural forms—flowers, apples, oranges or the potato—are popular combinations. But although the subject matter does not alter dramatically from artist to artist, the artist's treatment of the subject does—look at the variety of still life paintings and you will see the possibilities inherent in even the simplest objects. For example the work of William Scott demonstrates his endless explorations of kitchen utensils (fig. 1). For Braque, as for Morandi, still life provided a central anchor around which he developed his ideas. These ideas were based on a thorough knowledge of the objects which surrounded him in his studio and in addition, they were objects of affection.

Fig. 1 Still life can be successfully explored through the most simple domestic objects. In Winter Still Life, *William Scott pursues his constant fascination for kitchen utensils.*

Another great advantage of still life is that the object or the group of objects can, in most cases, be kept for indefinite periods. They can then be considered and observed in all their dimensions and you can consider the various approaches available to you. This is possible with other subjects like portraiture, but inevitably the painter will become concerned with the sitter's comfort. With a still life group there is no such worry; you are able to experiment as much as you require for whatever time span you choose.

As stated before, the still life provides you with the opportunity to select those objects you personally like or find interesting. You can then arrange them in a space that you have control over; you control the

Above · Still life groups can be deliberately arranged to enhance particular qualities that the artist sees in various objects. For example, in this painting called Studio Cupboard and White Chair *by W. G. Gillies, the vein formation in the marble table top is subtly echoed in the leaves of the plant, which has been carefully placed to achieve this effect.*

47

depth of field, that is the distance between the objects. Working close-up, for instance, allows you to avoid complex perspective problems and, with careful positioning, the light—either artificial or natural—can be controlled. Natural light is recommended for it tends to be much more delicate and produces far more subtle colour and tonal relationships. Try and place the group near a north-facing window where the light is going to be fairly constant throughout most of the day.

Once established, the group can be left undisturbed if necessary. For obvious reasons don't arrange the still life on the kitchen table. The facility of being able to view the group and paint it over a period of time presents tremendous advantages. The lack of urgency and the private nature of the activity permit serious experimenting. You will not be influenced by the fear of embarrassment to which most people in a classroom situation find themselves subject. You will also be able to allow time for each coat of paint to dry.

Not being pressured will allow you to explore and resolve what you are trying to achieve in the painting. Is it the influence of light on colour? The two-dimensional decorative aspects of the group or the three-dimensional structural aspects of the objects and the space surrounding them?

The other great advantage is a purely practical one. The materials can be left ready to be used at a moment's notice.

Keep your materials in good order. Remember to clean the palette mixing area with a palette knife and rag after each painting session or a muddy film could build up and destroy any attempt to mix colours with accuracy, particularly delicate ones. If you will be working each day the colours laid out around the palette can be left without any harm; keep them in tin lids, for example, covered by water—the water will prevent a skin from forming. If, however, a skin does begin to form, scrape off the colour and wrap it in wastepaper before throwing it away.

Arranging the still life and beginning the painting
Take the chosen objects and arrange them as swiftly as possible. It is easy to become too self-conscious over an arrangement, moving this way then that and finally arriving at a balance that is monotonously even. Try and produce something quite natural. Rather than fiddle too much with the group, move yourself around the collection of objects and find a position that you think is interesting. No progress will be possible otherwise.

When you begin painting, remember that patience is a virtue, that your decisions can and should be made slowly. You will find from experience that eventually such decisions will come more quickly and spontaneously, but you must not expect miracles overnight. Don't be too concerned about where you place things on the canvas, just be sure you incorporate all you wish in the initial line drawing before painting begins. Rather than immediately painting in areas of colour, map out the positions of the objects with a small hogs' bristle brush and a well-thinned colour, such as Ultramarine blue.

What you choose to paint is, in the last analysis, entirely up to you, and the activity should be one of pleasure. Anything that exists is a source of subject matter. Always keep an open mind as well as open eyes.

Analyzing what you've done

Before you can begin to analyze the results of your first attempt at painting, it is important to consider how you actually see things: to appreciate something of how the optic nerve operates in conjunction with the brain, and also how different societies look at images.

With the optic nerve, light waves from the sun or some artificial

Still life work (Table with Oranges) *by Howard Nicholls.*

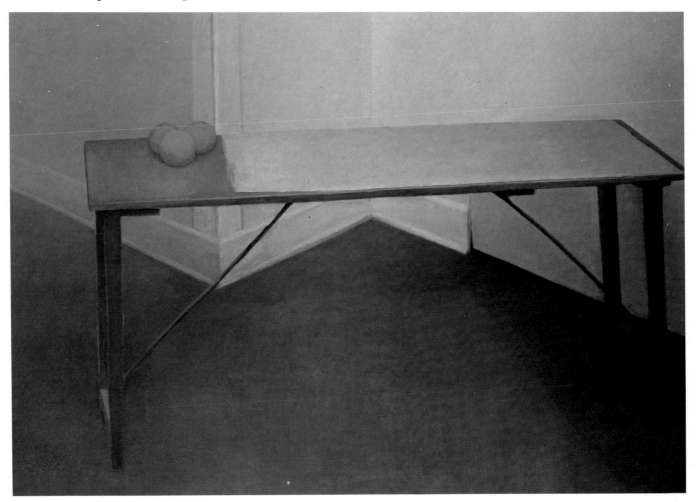

Right: Toilette devant la fenêtre *by Braque (1942) uses flat, vertical planes to strong effect. Still life is the cornerstone of Braque's art, and this painting is typical of his fascination with the influence of natural light on common household objects.*

light source are bounced off objects. Within these light waves are varying wavelengths and variations of brightness. These factors produce differences of colour. The light rays reach the eye and are focused by the lens on to the retina. From the nerves, impulses are sent to the brain. These impulses set in motion a complex set of functions allowing you to combine the visual information with information that has been accumulated since birth, through word association and example, into a comprehensive picture of what is identifiable as the visual world. This is, of course, a very simple explanation of the situation, but its implications are obvious; we are conditioned to perceive things in a certain way.

With a learning process by example the question arises as to how people view paintings. Viewing or reading bears a direct relationship to the society in which we exist. Some societies read from left to right, others the reverse. Twentieth-century European man's surroundings are far different to medieval European man's, as are their ways of living. Thus, when viewing a medieval painting it is extremely difficult for contemporary man, although appreciative of the painting's visual qualities and the artist's skill, to respond in any way as the artist originally intended.

An understanding of how and why you see things as you do will help in the evaluation of your achievements in oil painting. How pleased or displeased are you with the results so far? And what can be done to improve them? The initial difficulties will be practical: is colour mixing proving difficult? Has too much white been mixed into the colours, giving the painting an overall chalky look? Are the reds used too orange? It is worth referring back to the chapter on colour to review the examples of mixing. Is the consistency of the paint proving a problem? Used thickly without turpentine, or with very little, the paint will prove difficult to mix and take much longer to dry than paint with a high turpentine additive, and once dried the surface will be difficult to rework because of the underlying texture already established. No amount of scraping with a palette knife will remove the dried paint totally. Also the risk of damage to the ground, particularly if it is canvas, is high. It is wise, therefore, to begin painting with fairly thin opaque colour. This requires that the paint be mixed with turpentine and possibly linseed oil, although the oil will slow the drying of the paint, and give it a somewhat slimy consistency. Remember to mix the paint really thoroughly with a palette knife or old brush so that the colour will not be streaky as it is applied to the painted surface, wasting materials as well as time. Remember to load the brush well or, despite the tough nature of the bristle, the brush will get damaged as the paint is forced to cover more surface than it would naturally. For the beginner it is wise to stick to a fairly thin opaque paint consistency giving easier control throughout; it is also more economical. The density of colour will increase as layer builds upon layer.

Absolutely central to the success of any painting is the design or composition. This means the art of combining the visual elements into a satisfactory whole. The design reflects the selection and organization of space, colour, line, form and light as well as it reflects the artist's intention or reason for the painting. Lack of design suggests that all these issues remain confused. So to progress further, it is wise to persevere with still life as it presents those very particular advantages discussed earlier in this chapter—static subjects, control over composition, and light and comfort.

Fig. 2 In his painting Interior with Eggplants, *Matisse shows his fine skill in handling rich, highly active colours, and also an interesting sense of composition.*

Dismantle the still life you were working with and choose a new group of objects. Do not include an object, or objects, similar to those used in the previous attempt that proved impossible to cope with. Be patient, and a time will come when it will be possible. If composing a satisfactory group continues to prove difficult, look around the house or garden shed, for often casually placed objects create a most exciting visual proposition.

Another issue that could prove troublesome is the amount of colour involved in the group. Although bright, strongly coloured forms might seem attractive, twentieth-century urban environments as well as contemporary advertising bombard the retina with their brilliant and often violently contrasting hues, and it is an enormously difficult problem for a beginner to cope with such strong colour. This use of vibrant colour has its origins in the Impressionist, Post-Impressionist,

Fig. 3 In contrast to Matisse (opposite) Giorgio Morandi's Still Life with Bottles *deals with subtle muted colours and textures, and an uncomplicated arrangement of the whole composition.*

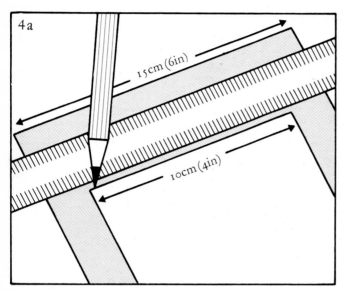

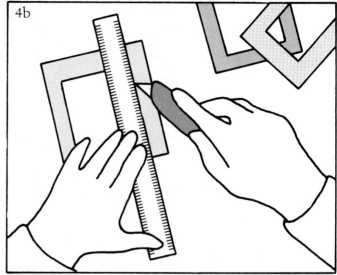

Expressionist and Fauvist movements of the late nineteenth and early twentieth centuries. Matisse (fig. 2) is a fine example of an artist who had the ability to control rich, highly active colours.

It is probably advisable to begin afresh with a very restricted group consisting of perhaps one or two brightly coloured forms balanced against a whole range of quiet ones, such as ambers, greys, cool greens and dark blues. This will help make progress toward a total visual harmony easier. The colours, although simple and perhaps somewhat conservative, will provide exciting visual and technical problems. Look at the quiet dignity of the Giorgio Morandi still life (fig. 3): a few simple objects are brought together in an uncomplicated arrangement of three-dimensional form and beautifully observed colour.

Having decided upon a satisfactory grouping you should now, before beginning to draw and paint, cut a number of viewfinders. These are small frames of cardboard with windows of different proportions cut in their centres. The window should be no larger than 10cm (4in) to 15cm (6in) square, and the surrounding frame roughly 2.5cm (1in) deep. The cardboard used for cereal boxes is ideal for the purpose. Measure and cut the window (see figs. 4a, 4b) to the proportion considered necessary. The 2.5cm (1in) wide frame will provide a sufficiently rigid viewer than can be easily held. If the frame is too thin the viewfinder will be floppy. So as not to cause delays in beginning the work, relate the proportion of the window directly to the porportions of the canvases or boards that you will be using.

Consider the photograph of the still life group in fig. 5 from which the drawings shown are derived. The first design in the square format is a deliberate attempt at bad design. The objects have been badly

placed along the bottom edge of the square and the total surface area has become dominated by the patterned wall behind. There is no sense of depth or three-dimensional space. The objects are swamped by their setting. There is also a strong movement toward and out of the bottom line of the picture surface that is visually very disturbing. There is no critical sense of balance whatsoever; the objects are simply stuck there.

The second drawing shows a very traditional arrangement. Three-dimensional space is important although limited by the shape of the table. Symmetry is established with the formal, straightforward position of the table and creates a quiet, stabilizing influence against the asymmetry of the objects on the table.

The third design is a dramatic change from the previous compositions. Three-dimensional space has been eliminated because the tabletop has been tipped up and flattened and almost entirely fills the canvas surface. Upon this seemingly flat surface are the objects. The painting is still about still life but the design is more positively about the interplay of the flat two-dimensional shapes of the objects within the painting's surface.

These examples of how things may be arranged in a still life should be a useful indication of some of the problems inherent in achieving a satisfying design. There are innumerable possibilities in organizing a design, of course, and practice is the most positive way of learning and gaining confidence. Also, looking at the achievements of others and relating what you see to your own experience will help in understanding the reasons behind successful design composition.

Before elaborating further it is important at this stage to stress that painting is not about copying. Consider the transitory natures of the sun, rain, wind, snow and light and it is obvious that to copy is absolutely impossible. The camera and light sensitive film can only register the amount of light coming from the object; that is how it translates the visual world. It is thus a question of translating all these elements into your own terms, then finding values with paints that in some way equate, when placed together on the flat surface, with the visual and emotional sensations confronting you. Consider the Renoir still life painting (fig. 6). Although words can be used to identify the objects, the painting is really an obsessional study of atmospheric light and colour falling over the various forms and surfaces incorporated within the picture plane. The effect of colour laid against colour is the subject of the picture. It is not a painting about roses—the flowers are purely the point of departure for the idea.

Opposite: A useful series of examples of how to arrange a still life. The main study (fig. 5) is the source from which three drawings are taken. The first (5a) is completely out of proportion, the second (5b) chooses a traditional composition, while the third (5c) radically alters the perspective in a positive manner.
Below: Guitar, Glass and Bottle *by Picasso shows his skill in choosing a few, highly evocative objects.*

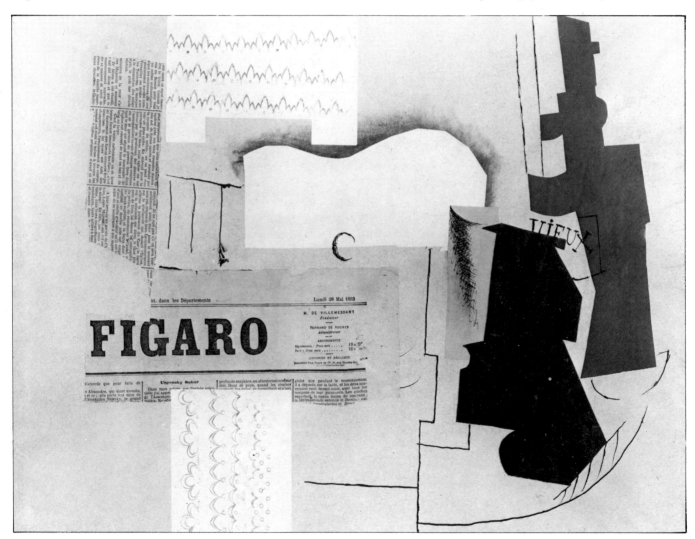

Now, try the various viewers: holding them before your still life half an arm's length from your eye, move them up, down or across until an interesting balanced arrangement can be found. Make a mental note of the important points that are to be incorporated and then arrange the easel and other equipment so that the viewfinder can be fixed to it by means of an armature while still keeping the chosen area in its frame. It is important that you endeavour to keep the position of your head constant as the slightest movement in relation to the viewfinder automatically alters what can be seen.

Proceed to work out a preliminary study of the painting in charcoal on paper to establish the main shapes and tones (how light or dark areas of the group are). The paper used for the drawing should be in the same proportions as the final painting. Endeavour to draw and place the objects on the paper as critically as possible. If things go wrong, and at some stage it is inevitable, just flick the drawing with a clean cloth or rub out the charcoal with a kneaded eraser or putty rubber. Then rework the drawing until you are reasonably satisfied with the results. This preliminary study will be really useful, helping to give a greater perception of the relationships within the still life group. When the drawing is finished, blow off the surplus dust and spray it with fixative at least twice. (Fixative is a resin and spirit mixture which can be sprayed onto the drawing to secure it to the paper; it is available in aerosol cans and in bottles.) Charcoal is a notoriously messy medium but perfect for setting out line and tone.

Since this drawing is a small preliminary study, it is quite easy to transfer the drawing onto a larger canvas accurately. This procedure is known as squaring up. (For these exercises it is best to use canvas paper.) For example, to transfer a drawing of say 24cm x 20cm (10in x 8in), to a canvas of 48cm x 40cm (20in x 16in) draw a grid of 2.5cm (1in) squares over the drawing. Double the dimension on the canvas and draw a grid of 5cm (2in) squares. The scale is now two to one. Then you simply transfer the detail from the squares on the paper drawing to the empty canvas squares. Use an H or HB pencil for drawing up the grid and be sure it is drawn as lightly as possible on the canvas, otherwise the grid could show through the final painting as many colours are semi-transparent by nature. Use thin paint (a neutral colour is best) and a small brush (a no. 3 flat or round hogs' hair is ideal) to plot the shapes onto the squared-up canvas.

The next exercise eliminates colour altogether. Use black and white and mix to make shades of grey to create a painting that is dealing strictly with tone. Tone means how light and dark things are; it is the amount of light reflected by the objects. The camera for instance operates on this basis. A few hours before beginning the painting, cover the canvas with a stain of very thin neutral coloured paint.

Fig. 6 Roses Mousseuses (*opposite*) *by Auguste Renoir is a beautiful study of a traditional still life subject, expressing a lyrical sense of atmospheric light and colour.*

Obviously, use a large brush to allow easy and even coverage. Place the canvas flat to achieve an even film of colour and leave it flat to dry. If stood up on end, the paint would run and create streaks. This stain will be invaluable as you begin establishing tones, for it immediately provides a middle tone from which to work toward black and white. Any mark other than the palest grey would register as dark on a pure white background and make accurate tonal judgements extremely difficult.

When the stain is dry, square up the canvas and work an outline map of the basic images on it, using the method described with a small hogs' bristle brush and thinned oil paint that has greater colour density than the stained canvas—something approaching black would be ideal. Using thinned opaque paint, lay in the large tonal shapes very quickly, endeavouring to find the darkest and lightest points first. (Remember the darkest tone might not be pure black or the lightest pure white.) This establishes the tonal scale within which to operate throughout the painting. Having laid in the large shapes in the opaque paint it is wise to allow the canvas to dry for a day, otherwise, for the inexperienced artist, the canvas can become a grey mess as over-painting and re-adjustments develop.

When the canvas is dry, continue gradually by adding more accurate shapes and tonal information to the large forms already indicated. To see tonal values with greater accuracy, half close your eyes and look at the still life through your eyelashes. This allows the light and dark shapes to stand out more clearly and not become confused with the local colours. For example, look at several objects that are of very different colours, such as a dark blue jug, a medium light red box and a light green book, in shadow (blue, red and green being the local colours). Because of their position in an area of shadow the objects will read tonally almost the same. Having completed the black and white tonal exercise try applying what you have discovered to the use of colour. Take a fresh sheet of canvas paper, square it up and plot the shapes onto a white ground as this will give greater brilliance to the colour being applied. Then, using opaque colours, establish the brightest colour and the richest dark colour first, leaving the intermediate shades and detail for last. If progress is to be made, a high degree of analytical study is required, looking at shapes and mixing colours as accurately as possible. This will develop a critical visual sense and result in a growing confidence through experiencing the medium. The most important point when viewing the result is how pleased or displeased you are; you are the sole deliberator.

Should you feel the results are disappointing, perhaps because the objects were too complicated, a simpler group can be constructed. Use some really simple shapes such as a cardboard box, a cylinder and a ball.

The tonal differences between the objects found in this detail of Chardin's still life study Pipe *and* Jug *are beautifully observed.*

If this seems to be too restricting, add one or two more objects that are constructed out of the three forms already in use, such as a funnel. The advantage of doing this is that the absolute simplicity of the objects allows the shapes to be seen clearly without any confusing overlay of decoration. Proceed as before—tone, then colour. The problems are identical to those confronted in each of the previous paintings—rhythm (in painting, where the eye naturally follows), colour, line, shape, but these are somewhat easier because there is no decoration or texture to contend with. Additional possibilities exist with this set-up, for having explored tone and the object's natural colour you could then pick up and paint each actual object a different solid colour with emulsion paint. The same group then takes on a completely different personality, although the objects are the same and identically placed as before. From this exercise comes recognition that a change of colour means a change of image. This exercise further reinforces the need for a knowledgeable perception of shape, colour and rhythm within the surface of the painting.

Finally, there is the additional complication of the ability of the optic nerve to switch its point of focus. The eye is an ultrasensitive piece of equipment that can focus intently on foreground, middle distance or background. When designing, a decision must be made on the optic restriction to be imposed, otherwise an obsession for switching from one detail to another, or indeed one part of the painting to another, could occur, and, as a consequence, the basic intention of the painting would be lost. This is probably the most singularly difficult problem to deal with. A way of combating it is, having set up the group, actually to write down what is interesting and refer to that statement regularly during the act of painting.

In the Degas painting (fig. 7), although the artist is dealing with a
large dramatic shape in the foreground which is crucial to the design
and helps build the atmosphere of the subject, it remains secondary to
the focal point of the dancers in pink, while the whole image reflects the
overriding interest in light and colour and movement.

Numerous alternative approaches to painting exist beyond an
analytical observation of a scene. For example the interest could be
toward decorative, two-dimensional movements and rhythmic interplays
of objects on a painted surface or, like the Impressionists, be involved in
exploring pure colour.

Elements of Composition

This chapter encourages you to try painting a landscape, and explains some of the problems of composition that you will no doubt encounter; picture construction, perspective, and ways of thinking about colour and its uses in such a painting.

The English artist John Constable (1776-1837) did much to popularize landscape painting. His painting, *Dedham Vale* (fig. 1) epitomizes what is for many people the purpose of such a painting: the capturing of an idyllic moment of peace and contentment in contrast to the noise and bustle of the average person's environment. Impressionist artists like Sisley in his painting of *The Regatta at Molesey* (fig. 2) contributed in much the same way, using a less realistic approach.

What is it about a landscape that interests you? You are not living in the time of Constable or Sisley, although aspects of their visual stimuli still exist—natural light, trees, fields and so on. But a great deal has changed in our present surroundings. Man's presence is more positively felt through more buildings, both domestic and industrial; electricity pylons and telephone cables that stretch for miles across most of the natural landscape. Ask yourself whether it is this aspect of the environment that appeals to you. Although it is a less traditional theme, it is still worth portraying. On the other hand, your interest may be aroused by the sense of peace you experience when you have escaped from the city for a day. The rich changing surface of trees, ploughed fields, hedges, pasture-land, domestic animals, crops of different colours forming a patchwork on a hillside—all these have been painted many times by many artists, but how you translate them into visual terms will be original and unique.

You will notice as you go through this chapter that you are given the choice of building your landscape picture either completely from your imagination, or from observation. It could, if you wish, be a combination of the two.

Observation plays a vital role in many artists' work. Even an abstract painting can be 'tightened' up and mistakes corrected by adapting information gleaned from observational work. But by no means think that working from observation gives your picture greater merit than if it were purely imaginative. You may even split your work into two separate compartments—perhaps observational drawings and freely imaginative painting. A good idea is to do detailed sketches from observation of features which are to be incorporated into your picture, and then take what information you require from them for your painting. Better still, carry a sketchbook around with you; draw in it, write down thoughts in it, plan pictures in it. This is, in fact, what artists throughout the centuries have done. Even in these modern times, contemporary artists use their notebooks in much the same way as Leonardo da Vinci used his at the end of the fifteenth century.

Working Outdoors

Working outdoors requires preparation and organization. You will need an easel as well as paints, brushes, turpentine in jars that won't leak, oil-medium, rags, a rectangular palette (for easy storage), a sheet of plastic to sit on unless you have a collapsible stool, and two or three small primed canvases of varying sizes. Also, considering the fickle nature of the weather, a sunhat and plastic raincoat would not be amiss. It might be worthwhile, before you set off for a vista miles from home, to view your own and your neighbour's back gardens as possible sources of inspiration.

Fig. 1 Landscape painting presents one of the most difficult challenges in composition. Constable was one of the first English painters to fully master landscape. Shown here is his fine study Dedham Vale.

For your first attempt at landscape painting try to avoid a view with numerous buildings that would necessitate drawing too many acute angles, at least not before you are confident you have mastered the rules of perspective, which are explained later in this chapter.

Beware of incorporating too wide a view for the shape of your canvas; this can easily happen when you are confronted by the huge expanse of a landscape. You would only end up trying to condense the forms to accommodate the canvas shape. Your viewfinder should be a useful tool in helping you decide your composition. A further useful device is the selection of a *focal point*. The focal point creates a natural pause in the eye's movement around the painting, and is thus a centre of interest. It might be, say, a group of trees that you feel are particularly important. You can accentuate them by increasing their size slightly or making the colour stronger. Alternatively, there might be a natural focal point in the landscape itself that needs no adjustment.

Fig. 2 Sisley's painting of The Regatta at Molesey *is a beautiful contribution from the Impressionist school to the genre of landscape, using a much less realistic approach when compared with Constable's work (opposite).*

Painting outdoors invariably means that you must work marginally faster. Finishing a painting in one day is certainly not wrong; you alone decide when work has reached the point beyond which you choose not to continue.

But remember that with one day's work you are only going to be able to achieve one application of paint. You will have to be confident about the decisions you make regarding colour and composition. Obviously, if you can return to the location several days running you will be able to develop your thoughts more fully. Traditionally, some artists, Constable among them, have done the bulk of the preliminary work outdoors and then returned to the comfort of their studios to develop the final paintings. If you are both patient and systematic you could confine your painting outdoors to the summer months, spending the winter indoors finishing the work started earlier in the year. In this case you may choose to buy a daylight colour-matching bulb for your working area, so that you can approximately match the colours found outdoors.

Painting and Imagination

Where do ideas for pictures come from? You may be lucky and find them easy to come by. Certainly they come more easily with experience.

The aim of the following pages is to familiarize you with the principles of landscape painting so that you have a structure to begin working within. Hopefully, by the time the painting is finished it will contain extra ideas and special touches of your own that make it into a purely personal picture. No doubt you will experience that strange blend of satisfaction with dissatisfaction that keeps you painting and seeking to improve.

Imagined landscapes have occupied artists for hundreds of years, although not always as a way of expressing a response to a beautiful scene. They offer a structure, an excuse for the artist to develop his own language of personal expression, which fundamentally is what painting is all about.

A major feature of most landscapes is the horizon. The words horizon and horizontal are obviously connected: on a piece of paper draw a shaky line horizontally across the top third of a rectangle. The result is that you have split the area into sky and ground. Remember, the horizon is in the distance so that anything painted near it will be smallish and will not usually stand out from surrounding areas. This is why the horizon usually appears near the top of the canvas, allowing plenty of room to depict the intervening space.

Later, when you begin your painting, you will probably include an horizon line. This can be very faintly pencilled in or, better still, painted sketchily in light blue thinned with turpentine (be sure it doesn't run!).

Draw everything onto the canvas with a pencil if you wish, but it's really not necessary. Most professional artists would map out the composition in line with thinned paint (often blue and brown), knowing that the exact shapes and colours will be painted over them later. Never overdo the preliminary drawing on a painting, it is a waste of time.

Foreground, middleground and background

Once the horizon is sketched in, it should be balanced by some vertical lines—perhaps trees or branches. If you wish, plan all this on pieces of paper which are in the same proportions as your canvas.

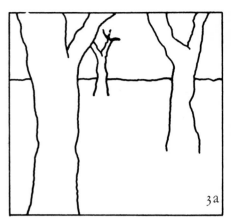

The trees will be of varying sizes and shapes. Those in the *foreground* of your picture—near rather than in the distance—will be tall, perhaps as high as the canvas (see fig. 3a). Don't make them too straight and don't worry about leaves and other details at this point.

Many people, left to their own devices, tend to draw their trees too small, as in fig. 3b. Generally, this is wrong and stems from a desire to give everything its proper amount of space, without giving it too much and thereby obscuring other parts of the picture.

There are good reasons for doing the trees as shown in fig. 3a. In fig. 3b an impression of looking down from above the trees is created and you may later find that you have trouble filling the canvas.

The main reason, however, is that fig. 3a more accurately represents what you see in real life. Look through your viewfinder at a section of landscape and consider the scale change from foreground, the part of the view nearest to you, to *middleground*, the space between foreground and *background*, which is nearest to the horizon.

Remember a *two-dimensional* or flat painting can only show an illusion of *three-dimensional* or solid space, so certain 'tricks' have to be used, and these help to create realism and depth.

Stand at a window with a view encompassing trees, buildings, cars and so on. Think of the window as your picture. Extend your hand at arm's length and use it to obscure a building, or any object that you know to be hundreds of times larger than your hand, as in fig. 3c. You are now well on the way to understanding the importance of foreground, middleground and background.

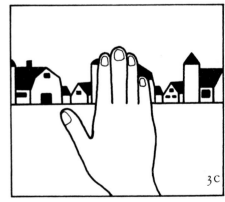

Above: Using trees in a landscape to express the vertical lines, and to demonstrate the principle of foreground, middleground and background.

Your ideas for the painting should now be expanded, so that you are thinking of enough things that will give the feeling of depth to, and reasonably fill, the space across the canvas. One hint: overlap some of the trees or other features. A picture without any overlapping areas will look flat and artificial. Look out of the window; you will see how many things overlap in life. Those parts of your painting which are being given priority should, at the most, be only partially obscured: this is the beginning of the process of selection which you will eventually find yourself following when organizing your picture.

So what actually goes into a landscape apart from the horizon and a few trees? Partly it depends on what you are trying to express. If, like Turner or Constable, you are fascinated by the moving shapes in clouds, you will place the horizon lower to give the sky greater importance.

Plan your picture initially from front to back, but keep the total structure in your mind as you progress. Work out the foreground first, since, if you try to create the impression of an enclosed woodland space with a very limited amount of depth, you will need less middleground and virtually no background, with a greatly reduced area for the sky. On the other hand, if you design the background first, with the size of everything reduced by distance, you could find that the foreground will later obscure much that you have already drawn.

Fig. 4 The foreground of a picture can be used to give a very intimate close-up contact.
Fig. 5 When viewing a subject for a landscape, it is useful to mentally divide the picture into several sections.

Imagine the painting to be your own field of vision, and decide how close the closest part of the foreground is to be. A bird perched on a branch could occupy nearly half of the canvas. Alternatively, it could still be the biggest feature and only take up one-twentieth. Individual flowers, leaves, branches, blades of grass, etc., could in this way virtually fill the canvas with foreground detail (fig. 4).

This creates an atmosphere of intimacy with the subject and will inevitably catch the eye. It can be contrasted with the grandness of rolling plains and distant hills which might be created by concentrating more on the middleground and background. Such a picture might cause a few more problems in filling up space and in relating one area to another, but these difficulties can, however, be overcome quite easily. Divide your picture mentally into sections as in fig. 5. Each section can be thought to contain the same amount of area on the ground, but on your picture becomes smaller as it rises into the distance. A panorama of nothing more than fields stretching into the distance could be constructed using this system of division. Without being too systematic, you can ensure that the unevenness in size found between fields does not conflict with their appearing to get smaller as they go into the distance. A further point to remember: draw the fields with sloping lines at their sides rather than verticals parallel to the canvas sides. Such vertical lines create the impression of climbing into the sky. This illusion occurs because, as mentioned earlier, on a flat two-dimensional canvas you are painting an impression of solid or three-dimensional space. The painting by Vincent Van Gogh in fig. 6 illustrates these effects.

For this reason, and for a better visual appeal, do not have roads or rivers going straight from the bottom of the picture to the top. Make them bend and zig-zag through all or part of the canvas, becoming

Fig. 6 Van Gogh's Crows Over a Cornfield *(detail) is an excellent example of how to paint fields—notice how he achieves a three dimensional effect.*

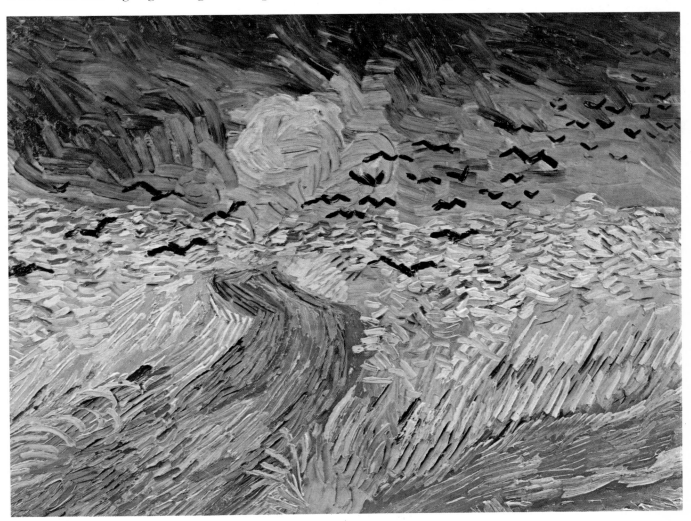

gradually narrower as they approach the horizon. Return to the window; you will probably see that you cannot follow with your eye any visible roads or streams all the way to the horizon. They will go out of sight before getting there, even if they reappear from behind a hill, forest or village later.

Incidentally, the snaking of a road or river is helpful in making the viewer's eye travel around the picture, thereby keeping his interest alive. In other words, it also serves to link features of the painting together. A road may pass through a village, cross a stream, or fork in several directions. It may climb hills or descend into valleys. It may pass from danger into safety. It could contrast the difference between urban and rural life: setting the scene for an industrial town which is gloomy and grey surrounded by refreshing hills and mountain waterfalls.

Fig. 7 There are several traditional kinds of methods of composition. Bruegel's Hunters in the Snow *illustrates the 'L' shape, which has a vertical feature balancing a horizontal, both in the foreground.*

Consciously or subconsciously, in giving one thought priority over another, you will start to create the 'feel' of your landscape. A quaint village in the distance, set near a lake and at the end of a mountain valley, must create a different impact to a close-up of some tragic scene taken straight from the news headlines of the day.

Some principles remain constant however, and you will not want to forget to incorporate some overlapping. Hills covered by woods may partly obscure a valley behind. Broken layers of hills will suggest that your scene is just part of a vast expanse of space, again enhancing the impression of distance.

You have so far been considering, fairly separately, the elements of a picture which comprise firstly the foreground, and subsequently the middleground. What you put into the background will not essentially be different from the middleground, although it is of course pointless to include details here which are vital to the picture's impact—they may be overlooked. Any background details must form part of the extras which give your picture more than just a passing interest. Paintings should appeal in two ways: first, they should attract the viewer's interest, and then should keep his interest alive; this is, in part, the function of the background. Hills or mountains in the distance may help contain the eye and stop it following a road or similar feature straight out of the picture.

Fig. 8 Another method of composition, used here to employ large areas to focus on a smaller, significant area is a rough foreground frame around the outside of the picture.

More about Picture Composition

Keeping interest alive stems largely from sound picture composition or arrangement, and most successful compositions have a *focal point*.

Diagonal lines, in the form of branches, roads, people pointing, cranes and so on, move your eye from one part of the canvas to another and to and from the focal point. If one diagonal leads to another, continuous visual movement can be achieved.

Look at paintings by old and modern masters. See if there are any recurring compositional features—the following three are most common:

1. The L-shape, with a vertical feature balancing a horizontal, both in the foreground. The vertical can be on either side of the horizontal. Bruegel's *Hunters in the Snow* (fig. 7) is an example of the L-shape.

2. A rough foreground frame around the outside of the picture. This will focus attention on the middleground. It is best not to have the focal point dead-centre as this can look artificial and boring. Fig. 8 shows how this feature could make use of large areas to focus attention on a smaller, more important, area.

3. The Triangle. This arrangement was much used in the Renaissance period, and its uses are still applicable today. Curiously it provides a circular motion for the eye, which counterbalances the more dynamic

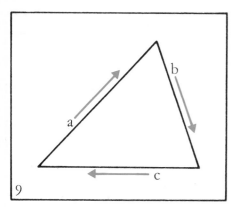

uses to which the diagonal is usually put. Look at fig. 9: line **a** could be represented by someone kneeling and pointing up to a figure, who in turn is looking down at something else along line **b.** Line **c** may just be a continuous line created by their costumes draping on the ground. *Déjeuner sur l'herbe* by Edouard Manet (fig. 10) is a sophisticated example of triangular composition combined with the fairly anonymous framing mentioned in 2. An additional element is the bundle of clothes. Probably a purely compositional device, providing a diagonal lead-in to the picture, this contributed to the storm with which this picture was received when it was entered for the annual *Salon* for established practising artists in Paris, 1873. The painting was rejected as indecent at the time—more probably for the men's calm acceptance of the naked woman, than for the idea of incorporating a nude into a work of art: a fairly commonplace occurrence. Notice as well how the horizontal lines break the triangle up into the more important foreground group of three figures and the additional figure of the woman in the background.

Figs. 9 and 10 Both these pictures illustrate the classic triangular composition. Below: Déjeuner sur l'herbe, *Manet.*

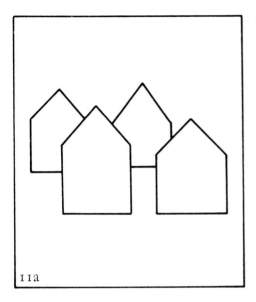

11a

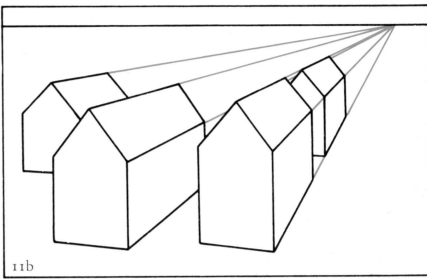

11b

Perspective

Another structural device which is used in the middleground and elsewhere is perspective. Mention has been made of the shape of fields, of not having roads climbing straight up the canvas, and so on. You should now learn the basic rules of perspective from which these points were derived. Without understanding them you may end up with parts of your picture looking absurdly wrong, but now know how to alter them for the better.

Compare the drawings in figs. 11a and 11b, both of which represent overlapping buildings. If fig. 11a has anything to recommend itself, it is in the context of design and pattern. As an approach to realism, fig. 11b is more lifelike and more visually satisfying—for two reasons. One is that it incorporates side views as well as front views of the houses. Try looking at rectangular objects around you, in your room and outside. You have to place yourself in extremely odd positions to view tables, chairs or buildings from one side only, without seeing all or part part of at least one adjacent side. We see everything at an angle, and in three dimensions.

Now consider the second reason for drawing the houses as in fig. 11b: what if the rows of houses stretched further into the distance? How would we achieve a gradual reduction in their size?

There are subtle differences between figs. 12a and 12b. Fig 12a achieves the desired result, but not at all smoothly. Fig. 12b, by contrast, achieves it more smoothly and portrays the basic principle of perspective.

Imagine the unlikely event of your looking straight down a railway line towards the horizon. You know the lines are parallel, but you can

Figs. 11a to 12b Various devices can be used to explore perspective, as shown in these examples.

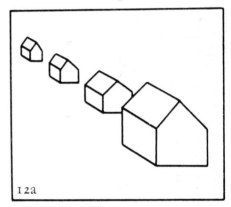

12a

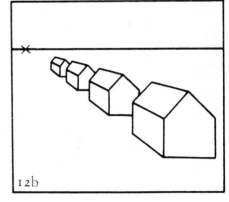

12b

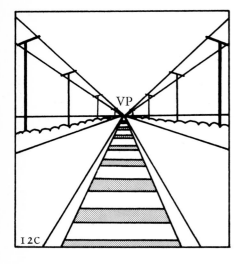

see they appear to come to a point (fig. 12c). The rule that governs this happening is that parallel lines going towards the horizon appear to converge at the same point on the horizon. This is called the *vanishing point*.

Returning to fig. 12b, we can see that the row of houses follows this rule. Don't forget there are different types of line in fig. 12b: including those which are not going toward the horizon and, in that diagram, are therefore not in perspective—vertical lines, sloping lines and lines parallel to the horizon.

Try drawing the boxes in fig. 13 in perspective by joining them to the vanishing point (VP). Notice the difference between the number of sides which are now visible. Why are they different? Simply because one is below the horizon, the other above. Just because the corners are con-

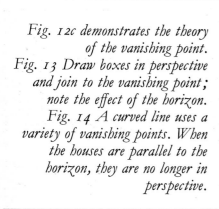

Fig. 12c demonstrates the theory of the vanishing point.
Fig. 13 Draw boxes in perspective and join to the vanishing point; note the effect of the horizon.
Fig. 14 A curved line uses a variety of vanishing points. When the houses are parallel to the horizon, they are no longer in perspective.

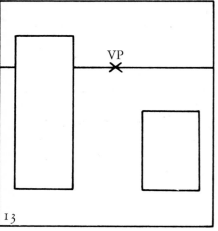

nected to the horizon in perspective does not mean that the boxes have to be the full length of the lines to the vanishing point. Looking again at fig. 12b we see the houses are cut into suitable house sizes, which reduce toward the horizon (things in the distance appear smaller).

For a row of houses or a street which curves, we use a variety of vanishing points (fig. 14), even if one of the vanishing points is off the picture. Where the curve of the road puts the houses parallel to the horizon, they are no longer in perspective. Let us now compare the drawings in figs. 15 and 16. You can see that in fig. 16 the house has two vanishing points. The rule here is that each surface that is turned toward the horizon has its own vanishing point.

Finally, remember that perspective is in evidence everywhere. Look

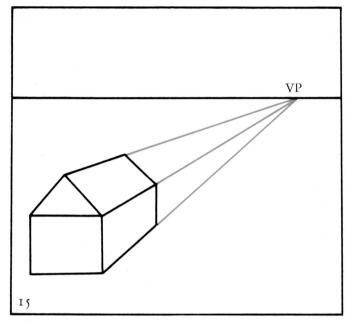

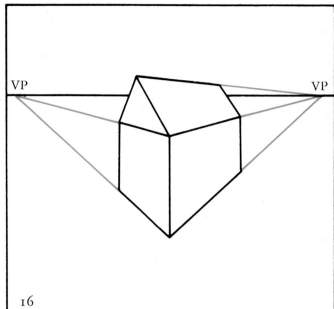

at fig. 17 and see how it applies in a living room; here the horizon or eye-level (the words mean much the same thing) is imagined. Notice that curved objects can be rendered in perspective too, and also that with anything supposedly divided in two (the window), the nearer half is depicted as larger.

Look for perspective in everyday life, especially in magazine photographs of kitchens and living rooms, etc.

It is not possible here to go into greater detail about perspective, a subject about which many books have been written. Visit your local library or bookstore if perspective is to play a major part in your work, but don't use perspective until you have mastered enough for your needs. Perspective is one way of making your picture look right, but in the final analysis, if you have achieved this without perspective you have still created a successful picture.

Putting everything together

We have discussed working outdoors, working from imagination, using foreground, middleground and background, and, finally, the uses of composition and perspective. Things will have been falling into place already, so that you will now have an idea of what your picture will look like.

Before transferring everything on to canvas, put it all together on paper first if you have not already done so. Three sheets of very clear tracing paper (in the same proportions as the canvas), placed on top of one another and drawn on in felt pen, should give an indication of how

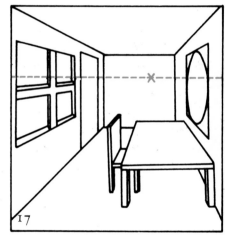

Figs. 15 and 16 illustrate the rule that each surface that is turned to the horizon has its own vanishing point.
Fig. 17 Perspective occurs everywhere, as in this living room. Make a habit of noticing how perspective functions in daily life.

well organized your picture is; how well the foreground, middleground and background go together. Is it too cluttered or too empty? Are the most important features prominent enough, and so on. The final piece of tracing paper should see the complete picture built up, after omitting or rearranging conflicting features.

Future pictures will almost compose themselves in your mind. You will find you can visualize increasingly well and will not need to separate foreground, middleground and background as you plan your pictures.

Size and proportion of canvas

You may already have chosen the size and proportion of your canvas. Some people (especially those working outdoors) choose the size and shape first and then fit a suitable scene into that shape. Others decide what they want to include and then choose the best proportions.

If you have trouble deciding what is best for you, consider the following points. Whether your picture is to be excessively large or else a miniature, you will need to consider carefully the factors of composition, contrast, balance and texture. So, for the moment, you should probably choose a fairly standard shape and size for your canvas. One which is 45cm (18in) square will provide a reasonable area to paint. But you may react against the regularity of a square canvas and opt for one that is, say, in the proportion of $1\frac{1}{2}$ to 1. This decision will automatically direct your activities to an incredible extent. In fact, it is one of the first serious decisions you will have to make (and then accept the consequences!).

Of course, commonsense plays a part as well. Imagine you are painting a picture of one of those gigantic South American waterfalls: you would be unwise to turn your picture sideways. In other words, a tall image requires a tall canvas. But a canvas turned horizontally can be ideal for many panoramic landscape situations.

What if you start painting and find that you have chosen the canvas proportions badly? You can hope partially to remedy a wrong decision about the proportion of the sides by focusing attention on the centre of the picture. Any unavoidable detail in the side areas should then be painted so as not to contrast too strongly with the background colours. The Cubist artists, principally Picasso and Braque, sometimes produced oval shapes in the centre of their pictures. A parallel situation on television is the use of a vaselined or blurred lens. This creates sharp detail in the centre of the screen with a blur at the edges. There is nothing to prevent you painting a blur of shapeless colours at the sides in order to increase the focal interest of whatever is in the middle of the picture. In fact this can be a very exciting technique.

The time has now come to start putting your ideas on to the canvas, but approaching an empty white canvas can be intimidating to many people. If this is a problem for you, try daubing some thinned paint on immediately, using a colour that is appropriate to the final image, with no concern as to whether it will remain in the picture later. Certainly the first stage of blocking-in very rough, biggish areas of the canvas in diluted colour should not worry you too much. By using turpentine and other mediums which speed drying you can paint over anything you've already done within a day or so. The first stage, then, need not be too precious.

However you paint, you stand a better chance of achieving a successful picture if you roughly block-in the whole painting first. Here it is as well to give consideration to how much tonal contrast you intend having in your picture: how light will the lightest areas be and how dark the darkest? Is there a particular source of light? If not, it would be as well to imagine one, even one that is off your canvas. In this way the direction of the shadows will be consistent. Similarly, you could decide on a time of day or year: shadows are longer in strong evening light; all shadows will be muted on a dull winter day.

Once these decisions have been made, take a small hogs' hair dipped in a suitable thinned colour (or use a pencil if you prefer) and draw in the outlines of everything you need on your picture. Some details will be left out at the preliminary stages. As stated earlier, you should not overdraw; features like blades of grass or ridges on a tree can be tackled later. That is why you are using oil paints—to create an effect that pencil drawing cannot give you.

Unless you are easily confused, you may even allow lines to pass through each other at this stage. It is only unsightly for a short period of time, and it can prove useful. Consider the 'visual logic' of your picture —whether things look right or add up on the canvas. Quite often a beginner will forget this visual logic when overlapping and will not notice that he has created an impossible situation. Look at fig. 18 and imagine the figure without the tree. His arm is unbelievably long! So, check the visual logic of your picture. If you have made a mistake, don't spend too much time correcting it just yet: merely repaint an outline, perhaps in a slightly stronger colour.

Blocking-in

Now start blocking-in (filling in) the whole canvas. This is the time when your painting will be at its least attractive; but it is essential to establish the major colour areas before you begin the details and other elements of the picture. Once the surface has an 'undercoat', it approaches being a painting. So block-in with diluted paint, thinned with turpentine or a quick-drying medium to ensure you can get to the next stage reasonably quickly. You may want to block-in all your darker colours first, to give a kind of instant contrast (or polarization) to the canvas. If you do this,

Fig. 18 Every picture must have a visual logic. Imagine the figure in this picture without the tree. His arms would be absurdly long.

just indicate which areas are dark by using greys, browns, blues or greens which are a shade darker than middle-grey. By going to extremes too soon, you could destroy the picture's unity.

As an alternative to starting with the darker colours, you might block-in the sky first. In this case, remember that the idea of a sky being blue is only half the truth. More often it is whitish-grey with greyish-blue patches. Don't put your brightest blues on to the picture too early. Be economical with all bright colours until you can control them. As with the first notes played in a piece of music, the first few colours will determine the 'pitch' of the picture. Similarly, too dark a grey will also dominate. Extremes of colour or tone can come later.

A good idea is to block-in the sky with three related colours of similar tone (say three basic blues, greys or off-whites, with just one slightly darker). Accept that these will change as you go on.

It is perhaps worth mentioning that, should you incline toward the use of brighter or more imaginative colours, your sky can be any colour you wish: green or crimson skies are not unheard of in real life. Even if they were you could include them as you are master of your own ideas. Extra care and thought would of course have to be given to the colours used elsewhere in the picture.

Cover the rest of your canvas in the same way. Establish three main tones—light, middle and darker. You can either block-in using colours which are related to the final colour, or in colours which are softer and more neutral. This method establishes a tentative kind of unity in the picture. You will then think twice before breaking that unity with a discordant colour.

Maintaining colour unity

Having started off with the whole picture in mind, aim to keep its unity throughout. Refer back to the colour wheel in the Handling Colour chapter. If your main areas of colour include all the complementary pairs (or some of them): red and green; blue and orange; yellow and mauve; or colours similar to them (e.g. *pink* and green), you are likely to destroy your picture's unity. You will see from the painting in fig. 19 that it is possible to incorporate all of these into one painting, but the problems are increased. Once you have decided which colours are essential, you can plan the rest to suit the unity of the picture as much as its realism. For instance, the colour of a tree is not necessarily brown. Trees are grey, green with moss, whitish-brown, reddish-brown and so on, so you could adapt their colour if desired. If you want a particular colour for painting, say, an elm tree, it is useful to know that one way to harmonize colours is to add a hint of colour taken from an adjacent feature. They will sit better together on the canvas and, if it is not overdone, both colours will retain their identity.

The natural division into sky and ground can lead toward either disunity or harmony within a picture, depending on how they are coloured. For example, an orange sunset about a blue seascape would need an extra unifying feature to pull the two together. This might be something vertical (a tree on land, a lighthouse). Alternatively, a pale blue-grey sky against a misty sea may need a stronger colour in the foreground to give it vitality.

If you find colour control a problem, limit yourself to part of the colour wheel as the maximum colour range for the larger features of your canvas. This may be as narrow a range as blue, blue-green and purple, plus their associated greys: blue-grey, mauve-grey, with perhaps brown added (blue being an ingredient in the making of brown).

A further way of keeping harmony within a picture is to make every colour the same tone. In other words no colour is lighter or darker than any other. If they are all to be light, white must be added to make a blue as light as a yellow. Conversely, if they are all dark, the yellow will need darkening, making it the same tone as the blues. Remember, however, that yellow is the most easily destroyed colour, and that darkening it may turn it slightly green or brown. This is an artificial method, especially if you lighten the tones. Lightening tones is associated with

Mountain Landscape (fig. 19) by David Rose is very much about the relationship of colours, while the rocks and mountains provide a loose structure in which to explore this.

some modern artists who use bright colours. It was used initially in the last century by Turner and then by the Impressionists who were all vitally concerned with the changing effects of sunlight. Very often they would paint in early morning or early evening light, staring straight toward the rising or setting sun. They would even paint in mist and fog. These lighting conditions automatically made the tones more even (provided the painter positioned himself to take advantage of them). These artists had a natural affinity with bright colours, one that contributed later to the momentum of twentieth-century art. Much of this century's art has abandoned or lessened the importance of absolute realism. Consequently painters have been free to experiment with the optical effects of colour.

Equally-toned colour has a natural tendency to give an ambiguous spatial effect. Its evenness, for example, tends to create flatness. On the other hand blue creates the feeling of distance, and red of closeness. Consequently the flatness is balanced by the artificial illusion of depth.

It was fascination with ambiguities such as these that inspired Turner, Monet and Seurat in the nineteenth century. Matisse and Bonnard followed with their particular interests in colour early in this century; the trend has continued up to the present time with the work of Albers, Vasarely and, most recently, Patrick Caulfield.

Since the development of photography, artists have been less concerned with pure realism, because it can be captured instantaneously on

Norham Castle, Sunrise *by Turner. The effect of painting through a misty, early morning sunrise is beautifully shown here, and gives an even quality to the tones in the painting.*

The questions posed by different effects of light and colour were explored throughout the nineteenth century, and well into our own era. Matisse uses interesting combinations of primary colour with a style unusual for him in his work Luxe, calme et volupté.

film. You can see that, in the case of the artists mentioned above, the link between them would be an interest in the different effects that can be achieved through a masterly use of colour. They are all serious artists, yet the latter ones have been concerned with design, composition and optics without realism as much as Turner and Monet were involved with depicting what they saw.

As you gain experience in painting, you may well find that many prejudices against modern art will evaporate. Not all of them will, since even some artists fail to understand one another; but you may gain a degree of tolerance for their work by understanding the problems that they have faced.

Returning to the question of the picture's unity, it is possible to formulate a rule for avoiding disharmony. One could say that a colour range covering the whole colour wheel, painted in dissimilar tones and with a lack of structuring, is a formula for disaster.

By avoiding all the pitfalls you may find you have fallen into the equally dangerous trap of creating a bland or anaemic picture—one that is 'nice' but uninteresting. Be bold in your decisions and let your boldness show through occasionally in your work; but at the same time remember at the back of your mind the question of unity, the totality of your picture.

Toward a finished picture

You are now virtually on your own. Unless you paint at evening classes this next, most important, stage of your painting will be done without being overseen by a teacher or experienced artist. Painting can be a solitary business and often many of the problems can only be resolved through experimentation. On the other hand, it is not a bad idea to join an art club or circle to experience some constructive comment and criticism.

Let us, as far as possible, be practical about the final stage. We talked earlier about whether it was feasible to start painting at the top left-hand corner of your picture and continue by working across and down. Generally, and this is important to the 'look' of your picture, paint distant features first. This is logical, since if you paint a tree before the

Landscape doesn't only encompass country vistas of trees and fields. An urban/industrial scene like Lowry's (below) shows how strongly evocative this genre of painting can be.

sky behind it, there may be an almost invisible overlap, making the sky look as if it were coming forward around the edges of the tree. Similarly, paint large areas before smaller ones.

Much has been said about the different directions your picture could take. Decide now whether you want to aim for as real-looking an image as possible, or whether you are more concerned with a decorative design loosely based on landscape. Choose whether you will paint each separate area with one flat colour or aim to create the impression of solid reality by using light and shade as much as possible. There is no in-between measure. It is strange that a tree painted in, say, two shades of brown will look worse than one painted flat or one painted in several shades.

Try looking at a brand new red car in bright light; you automatically accept its colour as red. Upon close inspection you will see there are several shades of red: in fact, where there are reflections on its shiny surface, you may wonder whether you are looking at a red car at all. Look again at the whole car. It is still undeniably red, its colour creating a total impression first that only on scrutiny is revealed to be made up of several other colours and tones. The total colour impression, in this case red, is known as *local colour*.

Ponder for a while on what it is that makes all these colours so different and yet combine to give an impression of 'redness'. This phenomenon is not restricted to brand new cars. The clothes you are wearing, the wall against which you are standing, everything has its own local colour which is affected by its surroundings, by lighting and so on. In fact, this is one of the ways we perceive objects to be three-dimensional. Stereoscopic vision without the effects of light and shade would be useless.

It is worth noting that before the time of Turner and the Impressionists in the nineteenth century, shadows were automatically represented by very dark tones. Shadows were not excluded from their work; instead blues and mauves, dark greens and browns were substituted for darker, more blackish colours. This lightened their pictures by comparison with, say, the chiaroscuro of Caravaggio (see fig. 7, Techniques).

Black, sometimes called the queen of colours, is also about the most dangerous colour to use straight from the tube. Pure black is not found in visible nature. Even black clothes are a very dark shade of grey. Try squeezing out a little black paint from the tube and then look for something around you that is as black as the paint. You will probably find this impossible. The nearest you get will probably be something man-made. Apart from this, black can easily kill the effects of other, lighter colours. To a lesser extent a dark black-grey without any added colour may also disrupt your picture's harmony.

There are, however, always contradictions in art (which accounts for part of its fascination), and you may find once or twice that black is just the colour needed to set your picture off.

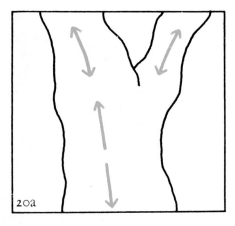

20a

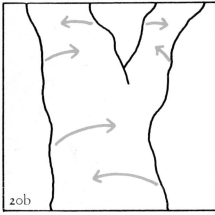

20b

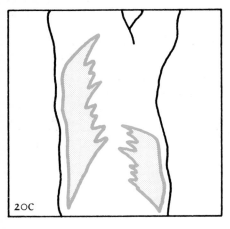

20C

Figs. 20a to 20c Partial realism is best achieved by painting the subject in patches of colour.

Always mix your colours; avoid, where possible, using them straight from the tube. Even your brightest colours should be mixtures. Colours straight from the tube, if used in large areas, will lack depth and be unsatisfying.

If you are aiming for partial realism at least, and consequently for a variety of colours on any one object, paint your colours in areas or patches. Don't just follow the contours of a tree when painting one. Most subjects can be painted in two directions. The tree (fig. 20a), which is basically vertical in its structure, will look better if painted in a way which also takes account of its roundness (fig. 20b). For this reason, many professional painters temporarily disregard the obvious structure of what they are painting. Once the basic colour is blocked-in, they might paint in patches of colour, using here a small dab of paint, there a longer brush stroke. There may be areas of colour which if scrutinized appear to be of a strange shape, as in 20c. Upon analysis, however, their role is clearer. The shape here is an ideal compromise between upward and curved horizontal strokes. By standing back from your painting you can inspect it to check how it works as a whole. In this way you may paint a dab of colour in one part of the picture and then another far away from your first mark. You may not choose to paint in this way, but there are good reasons for doing so. First, if you build up the depth of colour on one side, it will eventually need balancing elsewhere. Secondly, it is best to keep returning to an area, adding small refinements until you have built an image that may have literally dozens of adjacent colours.

As a mental exercise think about putting, say, twenty slightly different shades of red in an area 5cm (2in) square. Inspection of Monet's *Water Lilies* shows that he would paint dozens of very similar colours adjacent to each other. What we see in an instant is really the product of a great deal of time and repeated attention by this artist. He would continually return to one particular area, in between painting other parts of the canvas, adding a subtly different colour here, another there. In this way he achieved a final richness which is a veritable profusion of colour. It is of course not necessary to go to these lengths. Indeed, Monet's paintings are an acquired taste and you may yourself prefer to have less fussy detail by painting with fewer colours than he did. Undeniably, however, such paintings will first catch your attention and then keep it, making you look again. A real work of art should be relished or savoured. One day you may well discover a painter whose work captures your imagination completely. Such a reaction is different from admiring technical skill, although such skill may well be present too. Indeed, what is technical skill? Is it the ability to paint photographically, so that you feel you could almost pick an apple from a painted still life? Or is it the ability to convey in paint an idea or emotion which may be totally unconnected with realism? For the moment, imagine that you do want to

achieve a kind of realism. Two factors will be involved: first, the totality of painting and, secondly, your accuracy in matching painted colours to their counterparts on the object or scene to be depicted. A painted tree is an illusion; it is not a real tree. So, can a man-made product, your oil paints, be used in such a way as to match natural colours exactly? Certainly the relationship between colours can be matched exactly to the original. Practice will make your colour matching more accurate. The tendency when first trying to match a colour is to keep adding fresh paint to an approximately correct colour. Often the result is that you mix ten times the amount of paint needed, it gets out of control through being too thick and oily, and it may even then be the wrong colour! In this situation you are faced with a choice. You can temporarily make do with the approximate colour and refer back to it later. Alternatively, you can halve the amount of paint already mixed and then add another colour to correct it. Each time you add a fresh colour, split the quantity of paint in two, so that you are only altering a small amount. This should prove more economical, as well as allowing you to go back one

The Pre-Raphaelites attempted to depict reality by capturing every detail. Sometimes this created an opposite effect of unreality, as in this work called The Hireling Shepherd *by William Holman Hunt.*

85

or two steps should it go wrong: instead of adding, say, Alizarin crimson to a colour, you might return to it and now add Cadmium red. The ensuing change may be exactly what is needed.

Compare the colour you are matching with the nearest tube colours. To see what is required to alter it refer back to the chapter Handling Colour.

To match colours exactly you should have continuous access to what you are painting. If you do not want to paint outdoors, but still want to capture nature's colours accurately, you can compromise. A few different coloured twigs and broken branches picked up on a walk will give you a reference for tree colours as well as some tree shapes in miniature. A small piece of rock is different from a gigantic cliff in scale alone. The effects of water can, perhaps, be imitated at home by placing a neutral-coloured bowl of water near objects of similar colours to those you are painting; in this way the water will pick up their colours and reflections. House or garden plants can be adapted: their colours are the colours of the countryside, their shapes can become the shapes you require; woodland or even jungle. Flowers are easily obtainable for painting at home.

In his evocative painting Early Sunday Morning *by Edward Hopper, the artist has used shadows as a source of contrast.*

There are some problems which remain if you work at home. How do you paint green grass across two-thirds of your picture without it becoming boring? And how do you get variety into the colour of the grass? The easy way out is, of course, to avoid the situation and not paint anything with a gigantic expanse of one colour. Failing this, use observation to show you the variety of colours that one field of grass may contain. Otherwise, you have to develop a fertile imagination. For instance, it may be true that one field is to occupy two-thirds of your canvas, but blades of grass in the foreground of the field can be painted to obscure much of the distance. Because the grass is in the foreground you can use a variety of different greens, not all of them pure or bright, interspersed with patches of a ginger or brown colour to suggest earth. They may be twisted or bent because of the way they have grown, or because of bad weather. A few thistles or flowers may poke through. Clouds in the sky may create a slight shadow effect which breaks the distant part of the field into two areas of green and blue-green. Within these areas there may be other, more subtle variations of colour. The clue to solving the problem is to break the large area down into small, individual shapes and units which require a particular kind of handling, and thus remove the problem of not knowing what to do with a large shape.

Much the same situation is found in painting the sky. Here the colour range may be tremendous, but it must all fit together. There may be a dozen different shades of grey and blue-grey with an occasional near-white. Sketching or just observing for a few minutes at a time will improve your rendering of skies. To start with, perhaps you could go to extremes and tackle a sunset with strong colours (but not too strong) or a dull day with virtually no colour variations. The in-between type of sky where there are lots of colours, but ones which need a maximum of control, could come later. Paint the bulk of the sky with horizontal brush strokes; a sky painted vertically, diagonally or haphazardly will look peculiar. One tip in painting clouds is to remember that they hardly ever stand out in strong contrast all around. In other words, if a silvery cloud is *highlighted* against blue sky on its left edge, you may find that its right and bottom edges are *blended* into the sky. There may be a gradual series of colour changes within the cloud shape. There will be times to be bold, however, and you will need to include some strong line occasionally. Look at fig. 21, you will see this effect very often in skies, draped fabric and even shadows. One side is in strong contrast to its background, on the other it blends gradually. Look around you for similar examples of this happening.

All shadows are strongest where they originate; for example, a tree's shadow will be strongest where it touches the base of the tree and will fade gradually as it moves out from it.

Fig.21 When painting clouds or fabrics, notice that often one side is strongly contrasted, while the other blends gradually.

Paint shadows on foliage first, adding highlights where the light catches the outer leaves later. Don't bother with painting each leaf as a separate colour. Break the foliage down into three or four shapes of colour; one for the darkest area in the middle of the tree, a not-so-dark area to one side of the tree, and a very light area on the opposite side. These can be left quite distinct initially. When you paint dabs of colour for the highlights into shadow areas, or odd shadows into the lightest area, the shapes will break up to form an over-all mottled effect. This is much more economical and satisfying than painting every leaf separately, although flowers can be painted either in this way or petal by petal.

More unusual items, such as the colours of a bird, can be obtained by direct observation, or if necessary from photographs. Do not rely completely on photographs as a source of material. The development of your creativity or imagination is just as important as the development of technical skills.

So your landscape painting should now be approaching completion. When it is finished, make a point of hanging it. Do not be shy about your work; your paintings are something you have created that nobody else in the world could do. The only person qualified to judge them in the long run is you. You will certainly criticize your work when it is on the wall, and perhaps be dissatisfied. But you will discover bits in it which you like as well; often accidental parts are the most fascinating.

Try putting your pictures on the wall before they are finished. Tack them up with masking tape, prop them on chairs and leave them for a few hours or days. If you're busy with a job, or have housework to do, you won't be able to paint non-stop. It helps to keep the painting in your mind's eye as much as it helps to leave it occasionally. Let your living room be a bit messy for awhile: mull over your picture from an armchair.

It is difficult to sit doing nothing, just looking at your picture, waiting for a reaction to it. Don't force yourself to analyze. A conviction will grow on you that may confirm something to be wrong, or reveal what the next step should be. Play some music in the background to create the same 'feel' as your painting. Do this perhaps while you are painting too. Probably the secret is not to be too systematic; don't be scared of turning your picture upside-down or sideways to see if there are any obvious mistakes. It is surprising how this will work.

Once your painting is finished you will have already learned much about picture-making, both from the point of view of technique and of what makes a successful painting. Do you like what you have done—are you partly or completely satisfied? Perhaps now you will feel sufficiently motivated to carry on and find out more about painting. The next section takes what you have learned a stage further, and applies it to other aspects of the media, namely painting the human figure.

Improving Observation

Figure painting

Once you have attempted the still life and landscape projects in the previous chapters, you will be in a position to tackle some figure painting, having discovered much already about colour, tone, shape and composition. These remain the essentials of painting the figure, except that your powers of observation, or drawing, will now play a greater role.

Artists have drawn and painted the human form for hundreds of years. Even today it still occupies very many contemporary painters. Why is this? It is possible to attempt a landscape painting without once looking at a landscape. Your own style and sense of what looks right may be enough to carry you through, but in figure painting you cannot make guesses. The greatest artists drawing a person from imagination would probably not be able to do as good a picture as a reasonably good artist working from continuous observation.

Nevermore *by Gauguin—one of the painter's langorous and exotic Tahitian nudes.*

The human body is made up of a series of surfaces, or planes, which run smoothly into one another, and yet each of the planes will have its own exact shape.

Look at Rembrandt's *Woman Bathing* (fig. 1). Study first of all the outline, itself complex enough. Notice that it would be possible to trace the basic shapes with a ruler: that the figure can be broken down into a series of straight lines and angles (fig. 1a). It is always a good idea to look for angularity in the human form, but look closer and see how many curves are present too, just in the outline of the basic shape. There is a concave curve on her right arm, which, if it were any more pronounced, would look ridiculous, and yet it is just right. See how the opposite side of the arm is balanced by a very firm tensing of the muscles. There is much, much more to this picture than just a woman bathing. Rembrandt's drawing and painting style are compatible with the scene. He has created an impression of a girl who is decidedly feminine, but at the same time, sturdy. Compare it with the generous roundness of *Nude in the Sunlight* by Renoir (fig. 2). There the straight lines are kept to a minimum, enhancing the softness of her figure.

So, understanding the basic pose in Rembrandt's picture, look now at the painting style. If the painting were not in front of you, you would probably say that, generally, flesh colour is pink. There is not much pink at all on the woman's body, the colour is created entirely with dull creams, greys and browns, with perhaps a tinge of green. There may be just the merest hint of a creamy pinkish colour on her chest. Notice the softness within each area of flesh: the gradual changes of colour. The colour has several roles to play. It has to suggest the curves within the form (for example across the right thigh) by showing accurately where the body responds to light and shade.

Consider the difference for a moment between the roundness of a coin and that of an orange: the coin is round in one dimension, and can therefore be drawn easily on a flat surface. The orange is round in every dimension and is thus harder to depict on a flat surface. The same problems of capturing shape and volume are present in painting the figure.

Additionally, the colour emphasizes the intimacy of the situation. The background is in muted browns; the figure's shadows are in brown, too. Consequently, she is partly standing out from the background, partly merging with it. Remember that it was painted in 1654 and represents a very delicate scene: a young, partially-clad woman bathing. Rembrandt has handled the pose masterfully and yet delicately. There is a suggestion of private enjoyment on the girl's face, with her rich-looking clothes abandoned behind her.

Notice the different types of brushmark. The shift is painted with very bold brush strokes which remain visible for what they are; on the body

1a

The figures here and overleaf show the artists' use of straight lines and curves to define the complex planes of the human figure. Opposite: Woman Bathing *(fig. 1) by Rembrandt. Above: The body can be broken up into definite lines and angles (fig. 1a).*

they are blended more into one another. The *Nude in the Sunlight* was painted 221 years later, in 1875. Can you see that the setting is identical in concept to Rembrandt's: an intimate scene of a naked girl seemingly in the middle of a wood?

Now look for the differences. Renoir's painting seems much less discrete, more deliberately voluptuous. The creams and browns which go so well together in Rembrandt's picture have been replaced by pinks and greens, virtual opposites. This makes the figure 'jump out' of the picture.

Fig. 2 Renoir's Nude in the Sunlight *has an identical setting to Rembrandt's painting which was painted 221 years before. The two paintings make an excellent study in contrasting styles and methods.*

Look at the flesh colour. This time it *is* pink. But it is also mauve, blue and green in places too. Why has Renoir broken the figure up into a series of blotches? The reason is interesting in that both he and Rembrandt were passionately interested in the effects of light. But in Rembrandt's case it is lighting—the use of light to create a dramatic effect. Renoir is trying to say that the figure cannot be painted as totally separate from its surroundings because it will pick up the colours of those surroundings. So, ultimately, is Renoir's painting that different from Rembrandt's whose figure was integrally related to its background as well? Perhaps the differences are those of time, personality and society. The similarities are a reflection of what may be a constant in art: the challenge of mastering a figure or still life arrangement and imposing your own personality on it.

Structurally, Renoir's picture is very simple, perhaps deceptively so. The head is leaning towards our left, balancing the body's slight tilt to the right. If the head had continued the direction of the body it might well have created a feeling of leaning or toppling over.

There are a few straight, angular forms, notably in the arms and in the over-all pose, which balance the exceedingly soft shapes elsewhere. But there is nowhere a suggestion of tensed muscles; the feeling is one of complete relaxation, perhaps even abandon.

Just because Renoir's picture is softer throughout than Rembrandt's, do not make the mistake of thinking that it is less well drawn. The forms are all exact, the brushwork loose but controlled. A few dabs of colour are enough to suggest a wistful expression on the girl's face. The shapes of stomach, breasts and arms are all precisely observed, but they do not claim to be more important than the over-all impression created by the setting. Remember that when drawing or painting the figure, the setting is an important part of the whole. It can be painted precisely, as were many society portraits, to show details of a drawing-room or the sitter's possessions. It can be merely hinted at, as in the two pictures mentioned. You are creating an atmosphere or environment whenever you paint the figure.

Practise drawing figures as often as possible. Sit in a park and draw bits of people as they walk past—a successful figure painting is made up of accurately observed parts. Get your family to pose for you.

Eventually, you will have to decide whether you want to paint the figure nude or clothed. If you would prefer to paint the nude, you might enquire at your local library to see whether there is a painting group nearby. This would allow you to deal with the body's shapes and colours direct. You may even decide to form an art group and hire a model yourself. Painting clothed figures also requires an understanding of the form beneath. Clothing hanging on an arm or leg will often blur an outline, but will irrevocably be linked to the shape below.

Above: The Duchess of Alba *by Goya (1795). In portraiture, the background can be very important in conveying a sense of the personality and the texture of the subject's life.*

It is, therefore, very important to get experience of drawing the nude figure from somewhere. If you do not have a model you can obtain books on anatomy for artists. The changing curves and straight lines on our bodies are directly linked to the bones and muscles below the skin. Get to know what positions the body can and cannot adopt. For instance, a leaning pose will need to be balanced by a support of some kind: the arms resting on a chair, against a wall, etc. When using a model, remember to take into account his or her comfort. The model will need frequent breaks from an awkward pose, so you will need to chalk in the position of the feet.

Right: Nude *by Howard Nicholls.*

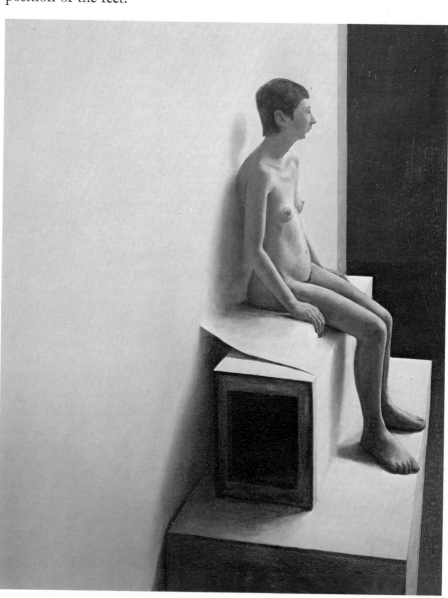

Your poses should be interesting. Don't just place a figure standing upright, hands at the sides, looking straight toward you. There can be a difference of stress between the top of the body and the lower part, between the left side and the right. For example, suppose you were given the title 'Depression' to express in paint. You might seat the figure on a chair, with its head in its hands which are in turn resting on its knees. This would create a hunched-up, curved-back, 'tight' feel,

When posing a model, make sure you look for interesting angles and effects. La Siesta *by Alsina is a superb study of the body at rest.*

95

The *human face can be an endlessly absorbing subject. As with figure painting, observation is crucially important. Examine the portraits on this page and opposite to see how painters use different techniques to explore personality.*
Right: Portrait of Chopin *by Delacroix.*
Far right: Mona Lisa *by Leonardo da Vinci.*
Below: Self Portrait *by Vincent van Gogh (fig. 3).*

partly balanced by legs hanging straight down to the ground. Try posing the figure with its weight on one heel, arms folded, the other leg contrasted by having its toes only just lightly touching the ground.

The human body in art is a potential reserve for action and emotions. Your picture could show tension, relaxation, joy or despair by the way it is posed and by the colours and style used in painting it.

Portrait painting

You may want to paint portraits. Here the problems are the same and again observation is the key. Never take shapes, proportions and angles for granted; awareness of these factors is the backbone of good observation. Check the size of one feature against another. Remember that a face could be divided into two equal or symmetrical halves; but it is at an angle to you, the features nearest you will remain roughly the same size and those which are turned away will be more drastically altered. They are *foreshortened* or squashed into a smaller space.

One eye in Van Gogh's *Self Portrait* (fig. 3) is immediately adjacent to the nose, the other a further eye's width away. It is more interesting this way and, since the eyes are still turned towards the onlooker, quite disturbing. This is typical of Van Gogh's work. He was a tormented man, tormented by loneliness and driven by deep feelings of inadequacy. The violence of his feelings is shown in the way the paint is streaked on to the canvas. But detail is not obscured. Eyelids and creases around the eye are minutely observed, as is the nose. Look at the shape of his head, how precisely it is carved out of the picture. The coat and background are impressions only, but still reflect his desperation in their handling.

Before you impose a definite style, such as streaked brushmarks, check you have captured the essentials. The eyes are the most important part and if they are unsuccessfully rendered, the picture will fail. Make them the first priority.

More about still life

With your new-found experience in observation you will probably return to doing more still life, landscape and imaginative pictures.

Look at fig. 4, the still life by Paul Gauguin. Like all good still lifes it is simple but bold; in its shapes it is fundamentally a realistic picture, but the artist has slightly strengthened the colour, so that the picture is basically all red and blue. In other words, the colours are approaching being complementaries. This produces the contrast between the turquoise cloth and the red sideboard. They immediately catch your attention and make you look at the more subtly-shaded fruits arranged on them.

But the turquoise and red have been modified, so that while the contrast is maintained, they are brought together by patches of grey-blue

Above: Self Portrait *by Picasso*
Fig. 4 (below) Observation is very important in still life work. Notice the use of colour in this still life by Gauguin.

and greyish-red. Look at the range of reds in the sideboard: from orange through to purple, and yet none are quite pure colour.

Set yourself a still life to do using much the same colours. You will see how the finished picture could range from the stridently bright pure red against pure (but light) blue-green, to the much softer mauve-greys against purple-greys.

Gauguin's painting is half-way between the two extremes. His fruits, basket and bowl fit in with the general colour scheme, but the fruit is much darker. Being dark and in the lower centre of the picture it stands out as the focal point. The basket, by comparison, largely blends or recedes into the colour of the wall behind.

Ask yourself certain questions to help understand how this picture, which is so simple, can hold your eye as a successful painting. Would the basket recede too far if it were not for the near-complementary colours of the pear and lime in it? What would happen if the fruit was lighter in tone? What other structural devices are there?

Perhaps one of the relevant questions you could ask is: how consciously was Gauguin thinking of all these points, or did he intuitively arrange and paint the still life that way? Certainly, he has avoided the pitfall of leaving his canvas divided into the horizontal sections created by the background, the sideboard top and the front of the sideboard. The shadows on the apples are right for the picture and are the result of accurate observation; but see how bold and original the shapes of these shadows are—they are almost a series of wavy lines. Many beginners would soften such distinctive features. Again, it becomes clear that the great artists knew when to be bold, when to be subtle. Of course we do not know how many times Gauguin repainted the colours to modify or strengthen them, but he did know when to stop, and that again is the mark of a good artist.

Try doing a series of still lifes, perhaps working on them simultaneously. Take two completely different subjects: some fruit for one—some harsh, modern, mechanical objects for another. See if you can paint the fruit in two styles: one to emphasize their 'niceness', one to give them a hard, unreal setting, but still making a successful picture. Do the same for the other subject: paint one version in a style which highlights the cold and alien nature of the mechanical objects. Then

It is excellent discipline to try to master the tones involved in highly polished surfaces and reflections. Shown here is a colour detail from The Marriage of Giovanni Arnolfini *by Van Eyck, shown previously in black and white.*

do a picture which gives them a warmth and acceptability they might usually lack. As you progress, you will discover that you are not just painting a copy of what you see. You are capturing its character, creating an atmosphere and stamping the mark of your personality on it.

Move on to attempt a subject which requires more precise observation: for example, reflections on shiny objects. Arrange together three things which are shiny in different degrees, and which take on some of the character of their surroundings by reflecting them. Perhaps their

outline shape should be very definite, such as a teapot with a spout, a kettle, even a mirror at an angle. Have some textured objects nearby. Control the lighting until it suits your requirements.

How can you make objects look shiny in your painting? It is done by an exact mastery of tones. Quite often you will find on a very shiny object that the lightest tones are next to the darkest, and that around both are the middle tones. Decide how different the light and dark are from each other, and you will be on the road to success. As an exercise, find something gold and something silver, even a pair of rings, and study them to decide what colours actually comprise gold and silver. You will find that they are made up of several colours which go very closely together.

Use smoothly-applied paint and thickly-textured paint appropriately, remembering that texture means detail and therefore focuses one's attention. Use thin glazes of paint perhaps to create a transparent look. Aim for variety in your still life by incorporating varied but compatible painting styles into one picture.

More about landscape painting

Look again at the following landscape paintings illustrated in this book: *Déjeuner sur l'herbe, Mountain Landscape* (figs. 10, 19 respectively, Elements of Composition) and *Water Lilies* (fig. 7, Handling Colour).

As you develop, you will either consciously or subconsciously follow a particular direction in your work. You may dislike strong colours such as those used in Claude Monet's and David Rose's pictures. You may just want to sit looking at a beautiful scene and put your admiration for it as naturalistically as possible onto canvas.

Try to get experience of painting both outdoors and indoors to see which setting suits you best. If you paint indoors you are automatically compromising between true realism and your imagination.

Which of the three paintings is the most realistic landscape? Manet's *Déjeuner sur l'herbe* appears to be, and yet the figures were almost certainly painted in his studio. In fact Monet's picture is the only one which was probably painted entirely outdoors. His imagination was perhaps the greatest, for after years of initial poverty he was ultimately able to build an elaborate garden at his home in Giverny, France. For this he imported plants from around the world, chosen primarily for their subtle differences of colour; even Monet adapted the landscape to suit his own particular passion.

Choose a subject for your next landscape which is capable of adaptation to different purposes. You might choose rocks and mountains or a view through some leaves to catch a glimpse of some mysterious or evocative scene. Paint two versions of it. In one of them set yourself guidelines which are intended to create as natural an impression as possible. Don't make any colour dominate unnaturally; give an impression of a particular kind of light—in Monet's *Water Lilies* we feel that we are looking at the sort of diffused, even light that might occur at five o'clock on a bright summer's afternoon. Decide on the weather: even if it is unobtrusive it should be deliberately so.

In the second version decide to be more 'modern' or expressive.

Right: Another version of Rouen Cathedral *by Monet, painted at a different time of day.*

Use colours and tones to create a particular atmosphere or mood. Or you might do a fantasy picture. Richard Dadd painted some exquisite pictures of fairies and elves. His painting *Fairy-Feller's Master-Stroke* is a miniature masterpiece. You might aim to express a changing scene and to paint spontaneously, trying to avoid the problems of thought and analysis, but accepting the disciplines of an emotional response to

Fantasy can be a rewarding aspect in painting, and returns us to the unfettered vision of childhood.
Left: The Fairy-Feller's Master-Stroke *by Richard Dadd conjures up a whole miniature world.*

Urban landscape might suggest drab tones, but in his painting The Pool of London, *André Derain has chosen a range of bright, bold colours.*

the landscape. To do this you might choose a range or *family* of colours beforehand and mix them together first, so that the immediacy of your response need not be diverted by the practicalities of mixing paint. To this end you could use a series of palette knives; several would be needed to avoid having to stop too often to clean them.

Some places, such as Glencoe in Scotland, are associated with events which leave an impression of tragedy in the atmosphere. A painting of Glencoe might use dark versions of the mauves and purples associated with Scottish heather to create a feeling of foreboding.

You may be retired from work and want to express the joy you feel in relaxing in your garden, looking at the flowers and trees you have lovingly planted. What colours would you use to achieve such a feeling of joy? It may be easier to answer the opposite question: which colours would you leave out? There may be no place for dark greys and black in your picture.

Do these paintings on something less expensive than canvas until you are sure of your continuing direction. If they turn out successfully, it is still possible to frame pieces of hardboard or paper.

Other directions

In David Rose's *Mountain Landscape* you can see that the rocks and mountains provide the loosest possible structure for what is a painting about colour relationships allowing the movement of your eye around the picture. Henri Rousseau's paintings created a private world to which only he had the key—an escape perhaps from the restrictions of his job as a customs official.

Observational work continues to play a great role in art. But equally, since photography and motion pictures were developed, the visual arts have been freed from the need to be about a real or conceivably real situation. This inevitably places a greater importance on the painter's own way of seeing and responding to the world about him.

Henri Rousseau's painting The Snake Charmer *(1907), inhabits a mysterious exotic world, both physically and imaginatively. Notice his use of horizontal lines in the water, and verticals in the plants to express the perspective.*

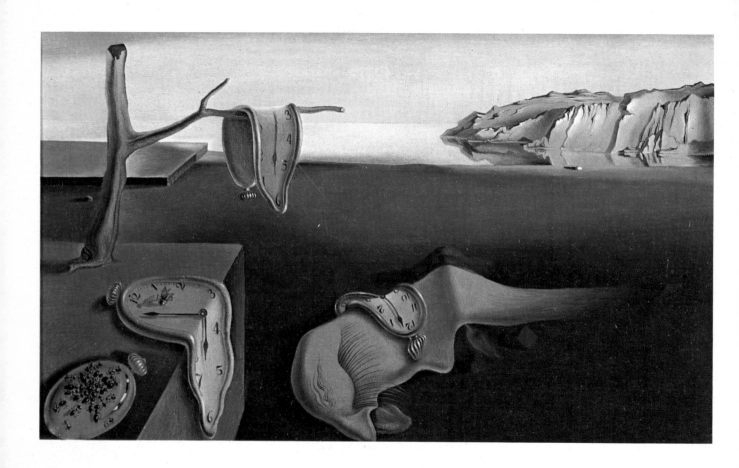

Surrealistic art depends both upon keen observation and technical expertise. The Persistence of Memory (*above*) *by Salvador Dali is a brilliant combination of realism and optical illusion.*

The Surrealist's work outraged many. The paintings of Salvador Dali have developed a blend of realism with optical illusions: comprising see-through people who seem totally naturalistic at first and then abstract. One of his paintings is supposed to be three separate and different pictures which change according to how far back you stand from the painting. His success with this approach depends on having the technical skill to achieve this ambiguity. Other artists combine painting with sculpture to make *kinetic* (moving) relief pictures. Some artists paint diptychs and triptychs—pictures in two or three sections or panels, each one having an independence of its own, but also relating to the other panels. Bridget Riley (fig. 2, Handling Colour) is concerned with optical effects.

Only you can decide which direction you wish to take. You may be radical and avant-garde, or traditional in your use of colour, form and tone. However you develop, you will need to learn some sort of technical control over your materials and some form of judgment in assessing your pictures. Apart from that, art is completely what you make it.

Techniques

Before you begin to paint specific subjects, it is important to consider what can be achieved in oil paint using the materials and tools that are at your disposal. The materials suggested in a previous chapter in this book will provide you with all that is required, and if they are used as advised there should be no technical problems.

Having already experimented with the colour mixing qualities of oil paint, you will have gained some experience of the types of marks your brushes will make, but a more thorough investigation will now be very useful. Try the hogs' bristle brushes with paint thinned with turpentine, turpentine and linseed oil and thick paint without thinners. As you work think about how much control the brush gives you over the various paint consistencies. Switch to the sable hair brushes and consider how they in their turn respond—which combination of brush and paint consistency is best to draw detail with? What sort of texture can you develop?

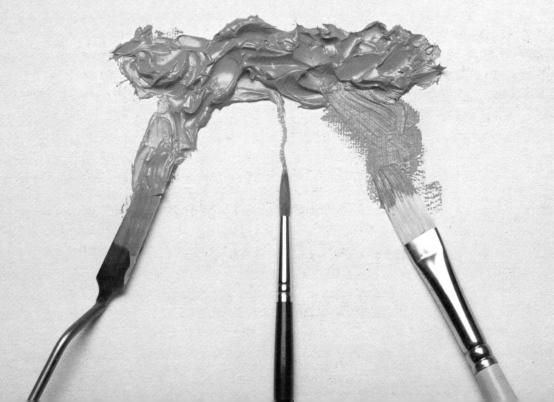

Fig. 1 The painting knife can be a very effective way of applying paint: Josef Albers used knife application in his series Homage to the Square.

Don't forget the painting knife. You will probably find that the paint must be used without thinners so that it will not drip off the knife or the canvas. Beyond this, a great variety of marks and textures can be developed. Josef Albers used a knife application in his series *Homage to the Square*. The painting in fig. 1 is part of this series.

The simple techniques described in this chapter will provide a basis from which to develop your own personal approach to oil painting methods. One thing to remember, no matter what technique you adopt, is to allow time for drying between each day's work. Otherwise in the end the paint will crack. Thinned oil paint will dry more quickly than paint straight from the tube, and drying agents will be useful.

Impasto
Impasto is the name given to the technique of applying thick paint which may have been slightly thinned, although it is more likely to be used at tube consistency.

With this technique, thorough mixing is important or unpleasant streaking will result. Use a palette knife for this purpose and be sure that a sufficient amount of paint has been mixed for a given area—otherwise you could be faced with the difficult task of mixing a fresh batch of paint identical to the first.

Apply the paint either with a brush or a painting knife depending on the type of the surface you wish to develop. Thick, heavily applied paint can look extremely attractive but use the technique with caution. Try not to be influenced by the thought that you have used a great deal of paint and so it must be all right. View the results in terms of the painting and whether it works in visual terms or not. The rich textural surface will catch the light and become quite active visually, so consequently such an application is not suitable for quiet zones or deep shadow areas. However, if you are dissatisfied with the result the area can be removed even a day later (unless driers have been added).

Always endeavour to apply the colour directly to the given area and try to avoid too much floundering around or the areas will start intermixing, possibly creating a muddy sludge and destroying all vitality of mark and colour. By adding drying agents to the paints you will be able to work fairly regularly. When the impasto is dry, consider the possibilities of glazing over the painted surface. Some quite stunning results can be achieved. Compare the detail from the painting by Turner (fig. 2), who often used impasto in conjunction with glazing, with the de Kooning (fig. 3), where the paint surface is built up with direct gestural marks of thickly applied paint. Obviously, such an active

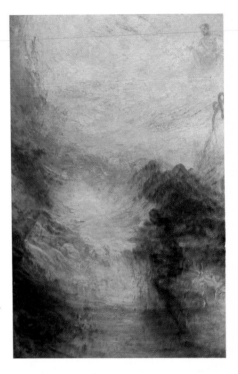

Impasto involves a very thick application of paint, and is a technique which should be used very carefully to maintain the liveliness of the colours. In his painting Light and Colour, *fig. 2, a detail of which is shown above, Turner combines impasto with a glazed surface to achieve really glowing effects.*

Fig. 3 (left), Secretary *by Willem de Kooning, 1948 is a highly energetic work in the Abstract Expressionist tradition. The paint is applied directly and vividly, achieving an effect of great spontaneity.*

Fig. 4 In complete contrast to the de Kooning painting on the previous page, David Inshaw's Remembering mine the loss is not the blame, *creates an atmosphere of total peace and timelessness, with very carefully controlled colours and surfaces.*

surface gives energy and vitality to the subject. This approach would be totally alien to the sense of peace in David Inshaw's painting titled 'Remembering mine the loss is not the blame'. Here the surfaces are controlled in a careful and restricted way, both in terms of colour and the fine application of the paint.

Glazing

Glazing is a popular traditional technique, used extensively by the Old Masters as a finishing-off process over a tempera underpainting (tempera is the name given to pigment mixed with egg yolk used as a binder;

it was widely used by medieval painters before the advent of oil paints) to give richness of shadow and luminosity of colour. Gradually, oil became the only medium used, but paint application remained methodical as the works were highly complicated pieces of design where everything was clearly established at the drawing and underpainting stage. Little intermixing of colour occurred, and richness and tonality were achieved through many carefully applied layers of glazing. Glazing is essentially a very thin film of colour evenly applied to the surface of the painting, preferably with a soft brush (a sable or ox-hair is ideal). Beware of thinning the pigments with turpentine only, as the addition of linseed oil is essential to help the paint retain its pliability.

Before trying out the technique on a painting, explore how the process responds to various surfaces and colours. Glaze over impasto, scumbling (see below), pale tints (that is, colours mixed with white) and rich dark colours, taking note of the changes that occur. Be aware that some colours are denser and more opaque than others and will require a great deal of thinning; this in turn will influence the drying time.

Glazing can be used throughout the painting process and, for the beginner who wishes for fairly immediate results, it will initially prove a slow process. However, glazing can be used in small areas too soon to achieve what one colour alone would not: deep shadows, reflections in a

The Agony in the Garden (left) by El Greco is an excellent example of glazing. Here he has used cadmium red as the final glaze, which gives a particular vibrancy to the white underpainting on the robes.

mirror or on water and glassware are just a few of the subjects that lend themselves to this technique. Though, technically speaking, it is not glazing in the absolute sense of the word, the work of Poliakoff (fig. 5) uses a technique of fine layers of paint in which the underlying colours profoundly influence the top colour. This method is somewhere between glazing and scumbling.

Scumbling

Scumbling is the name given to a technique of freely brushing rather dry paint that is either opaque or semi-transparent, depending on the nature of the pigment, over a coloured ground, thus allowing the underpainting to break through. A coarse textured ground is best for this technique for, as the brush is dragged over the surface, the paint will be transferred to the high points only. The result is an overlay of colour with a broken surface that gives added sparkle to the picture surface. Scumbling is useful for areas such as sky, middle distance landscapes and interiors through which light is filtering. If you ever consider painting a picture of a sunlit sea, for example, where light (playing across the surface of the water) would be an important part of the composition this technique could be used to portray this effect. Fig. 6 is an example of scumbling.

Fig. 6 Scumbling, the application of dry paint over a coloured ground is used in this painting Honeycomb Still Life *by William Scott.*

Chiaroscuro

Chiaroscuro is an Italian word used to describe the technique of constructing a painting on the basis of strong lights and darks. The technique was used extensively by the Old Masters to help establish the sense of 3D form. Caravaggio in the early seventeenth century developed a very organized system of chiaroscuro, and the painting in fig. 7 is an example of his work. If you decide to paint in this manner you will need a strong directional light; spotlights are ideal as the light source is then fixed and constant.

Staining

Staining is the free application of thinned oil colour to unprimed canvas. It is used by some artists such as Helen Frankenthaler (fig. 8) and can produce exciting visual images. It is technically unsound, however, because the oil can rot unprimed canvas, and the painting may not have such a long canvas life as traditional oil paintings can expect.

Fig. 7 Chiaroscuro is the technique often used by the Old Masters to construct a painting on the basis of very strong contrasts of light and dark colours. The Calling of St. Matthew (*below*) *by Caravaggio, c. 1597 is a typical example of the tradition.*

Flat opaque surfaces

The middle twentieth century has seen a massive expansion of abstract painting, much of which relies on superbly applied flat opaque colour surfaces. The painting in fig. 9 by Stuart Davis shows the application of this technique.

This might seem a straightforward proposition, applying several layers of colour evenly, one over the other, but it will work effectively only if the colour is truly opaque. Many oil colours have semi-transparent qualities; it is best therefore to first mask out the area to be painted with masking tape and then underpaint it with a tint of the final colour to be applied i.e. the colour plus white. This will provide an overall constant opaqueness. Make sure that the tint it not too far removed from the pure

Fig. 8 Staining is a technique which involves applying thinned oil colour directly onto unprimed canvas. Used imaginatively it can produce very exciting visual effects as Helen Frankenthaler's painting Mountains and Sea *(1952) brilliantly demonstrates.*

Fig. 9 In his painting The Paris Bit, *Stuart Davis uses flat opaque colour surfaces.*

colour, though, otherwise its very whiteness will break through, giving the final layer of colour an optically uneven visual effect. This particularly applies to Alizarin crimson which is very transparent. The tint should be of a smooth creamy consistency when applied and not thin or it will be insufficiently opaque; also, the paint would probably bleed under the masking tape.

Always use a large soft brush and endeavour to work away from the taped edges thus avoiding unsightly ridges. As with all painting, but particularly when working with large flat areas of pure colour or when glazing, the priming must be immaculate to allow for even application and drying.

If you wish to paint a crisp edge without the aid of masking tape, you could use a ruler to act as a guideline. Don't lay it flat on the canvas, but hold it 30° away from the surface. It should provide the guidance you require, for example in outlining the crisp horizontal edge of a table in a still-life group or the edge of a building. This technique requires fairly thin paint and a pointed sable brush. You can then paint the flat surface you require up to the established line. This system is also useful for picking out linear detail, such as fences or railings, or a view through a window where the frame is included in the subject. Few of us have rock-steady hands!

Left: Cataract 5 *by Bridget Riley (emulsion on canvas), 1967.*

Stippling

Stippling is the name given to the technique of building up areas of colour with small marks. A small round hogs' bristle brush is ideal for this purpose. The texture that results could be used in conjunction with glazes, impasto or other techniques—for example, consider an immaculately cut lawn such as the putting green of a golf course, surrounded by trees and unkept grass. A controlled fine stippling set against impasto and scumbling might ideally establish the visual contrast that exists. Bear in mind that this style of dotting brushwork is a monotonous process, so don't try rushing it. Explore different sized round brushes of varying stiffness; these will influence the final mark. If you want to overlay another colour allow the first to dry.

The pointillist technique of Seurat and his fellow Neo-Impressionists is essentially one of stippling, and it can certainly produce an interesting optical colour mix when controlled. Look closely at the Signac painting in fig. 8, in the chapter on Handling Colour. By placing dots of blue and yellow side by side the colours appear to mix optically and become green. So not only do the dots provide a bright shimmering surface texture, they serve as colour mixes.

Drawing upon your experiences so far, how you decide to use the medium is entirely up to you. Try to remember the simple rules of using thoroughly clean brushes at all times. Should the palette become choked with paint, remove the excess with a palette knife. Make sure the turpentine and oil are clean or the results of the exercises and subsequent paintings will be seriously impaired. Follow the simple advice given and the colours, surfaces and tools at your disposal will operate satisfactorily.

Below: Composition No. 7 *by Kandinsky (1913). Once you have mastered the basic techniques, you can explore lots of painting styles with complete freedom.*

The Finished Painting

Decorative surrounds occur in the very earliest of visual work: Roman mosaics had decorative friezes that at once both separated one image from another and interlinked them. The richly gilded frames of Gothic altarpieces strongly reflect the strict architectural order of their environment. During the Renaissance, the inter-relationship between architecture and mural was often enhanced by painted architectural motifs within the mural. This is best seen in Michelangelo's Sistine Chapel ceiling; the whole sequence of images is bound together with painted architectural frames (friezes). Several centuries later, the Neo-Impressionist painter Seurat actually experimented with pointillist hand-painted frames for some of his work, so concerned was he about the issue.

Below left: Roman wall paintings often had their own friezes.
Below: Architecture and mural are perfectly combined in the Sistine chapel.

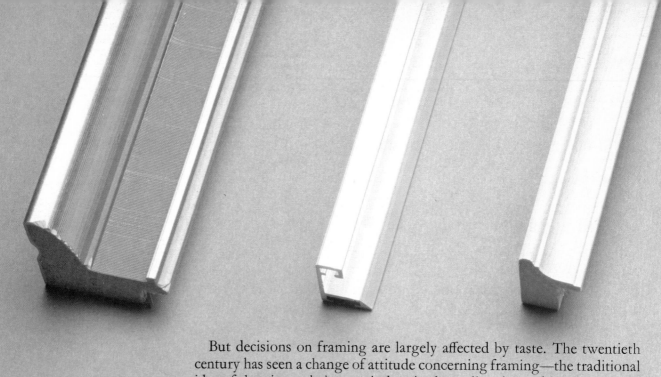

But decisions on framing are largely affected by taste. The twentieth century has seen a change of attitude concerning framing—the traditional idea of the picture being a window in the wall, enhanced by the use of a frame, was challenged by the Cubists who reversed the traditional format. Today, immense variations occur and often paintings that were initially conceived of without a frame, like the work of Morris Louis seem to have had the original critical sense of shape and space altered by the addition of frames, no matter how discreet they might be.

Added to the aesthetic issues involved in framing, is the simple practical one of protection. In transit or storage, corners and surfaces of painted canvases can be damaged. The frame physically protects the work, both corners and surface, for it is usual for the frame to project above the surface. With work carried out on paper it is all the more

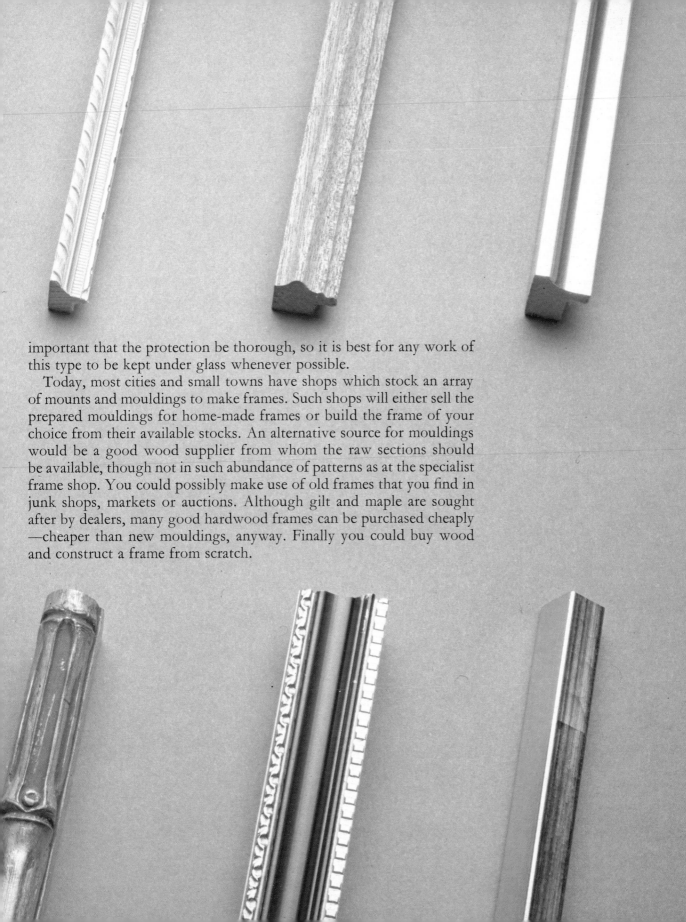

important that the protection be thorough, so it is best for any work of this type to be kept under glass whenever possible.

Today, most cities and small towns have shops which stock an array of mounts and mouldings to make frames. Such shops will either sell the prepared mouldings for home-made frames or build the frame of your choice from their available stocks. An alternative source for mouldings would be a good wood supplier from whom the raw sections should be available, though not in such abundance of patterns as at the specialist frame shop. You could possibly make use of old frames that you find in junk shops, markets or auctions. Although gilt and maple are sought after by dealers, many good hardwood frames can be purchased cheaply —cheaper than new mouldings, anyway. Finally you could buy wood and construct a frame from scratch.

By far the simplest solution is to have the work framed for you, but this can be expensive, and arriving at a satisfactory solution can be difficult. It is all too easy to rush in and buy what seems to be a beautiful frame only to find afterwards that it totally dominates or is not at all sympathetic to the painting. Always look carefully at what is available within the context of the work you want framed. In fact, easily the most satisfactory method is to take the work you wish to be framed along to the shop and try the various different types of frame on it. The sample displays of moulding sections can be really misleading otherwise: how can you envisage what the final frame will look like, particularly if you are to include inserts? Look at the made-up frames on display, they will be more helpful in making a decision.

If you intend to construct your own frame then you will find that the materials you require differ little from the selection for stretcher making, (dealt with in the chapter on materials) with the addition of some small wooden blocks and countersink nails. The first consideration is what

type of frame will suit the painting: a simple surround of plain wood that butts up against the edge of the painting, or a coloured mount around the picture and protective glass over it?

These issues are dictated to some extent by the size of the work to be framed. The larger the work the simpler the frame, because the work has sufficient scale for it to exist in the average domestic space and be viewed comfortably without much support from a frame. If a work is tiny it can be completely lost on a wall, particularly if it is competing with other works. In this case, the frame must provide sufficient impact to catch the viewer's eye and it must also be sympathetic to the work. The nature of the painting, whether landscape, portrait, still life, bright and lively or dark, has a profound bearing on the choice of frame and, for example, it would be unwise to put a bright, ornate frame around a very dark small painting; you would only see the frame.

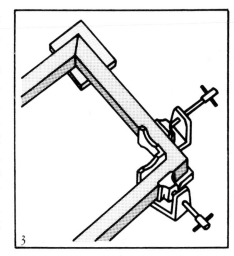

3

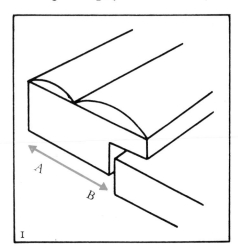

1

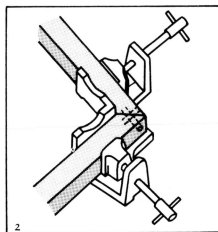

2

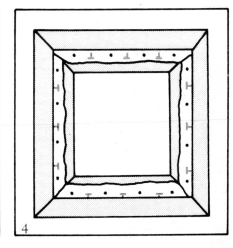

4

Constructing a simple frame with back-bend moulding

First carefully check the dimensions of the painting. All too often inaccurate measurement leads to additional expenditure on moulding.

To ensure a perfect fit, all corners must be cut at 45°, and although the mitre clamp should hold the saw vertically, cut steadily and don't force the saw or it could move slightly off the vertical. This would ruin the angle and present problems when joining. Cut the moulding into the four lengths required as for making a stretcher. The lengths are determined by two factors: the dimensions of the canvas plus twice the width of the moulding. That does not mean the *total* width of the moulding—you exclude the part that overlaps the canvas. In other words, looking at fig. 1, it is AB x 2 + the canvas length.

Be absolutely sure that the width is measured accurately or the frame and canvas will not fit correctly. To join the corners use a clear-drying wood adhesive and slender round countersink nails.

Constructing an insert (right).
Fig. 5 Use hardwood with a 45°
bevel on one edge.
Fig. 6 Attaching a small ridge
to the underside back edge of the
insert.
Opposite: Many Victorian
paintings had very ornate frames.
James Collinson's sentimental
study The Empty Purse *is an*
excellent example of this style of
framing.

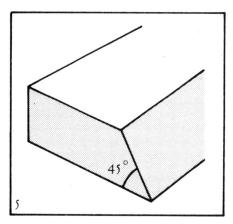

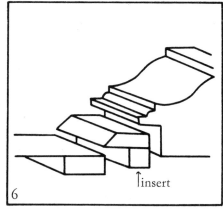

insert

Make sure that the angles fit together perfectly and then apply glue to each cut edge. Clamp the corners together in the right-angle clamp and drill a small hole through the edge of one piece, and just into the other (fig. 2). Knock in the nail two-thirds of its length. Repeat the procedure on the other piece, making sure the nails do not collide. Remember, the drill bit needs to be fractionally smaller than the nail to ensure a rigid joint. Under no circumstances run nails directly into the wood; always drill a small hole first. Repeat with the three remaining corners. Always support the corners not in the clamp during the construction with pieces of wood the same thickness as the clamp base, or the frame's weight could open up the freshly glued and nailed joints (fig. 3). Wipe away any surplus glue.

If constructing a large frame that has more flexibility it will be necessary to support the straight as well as the corners while joining is in progress. When the glue is dry, countersink the nails and use a wood filler to conceal the hollows. If your cutting has been inaccurate try to align the front face and fill in the back edge where it obviously will not show.

Place the frame face down on an old blanket to avoid damage to the facing (many manufactured frame surfaces are very fragile), slot in the canvas and pin by running several small nails into the inside back edge of the frame (fig. 4).

Complete the framing by gluing heavy-duty brown paper over the back of the frame and stretcher giving a tidy finish that keeps the dust out. This frame type would be ideal for medium-size paintings 51cm x 76cm (20in x 30in) up to 102cm x 127cm (40in x 50in).

For a small painting, as already suggested, a more substantial width of frame is visually necessary. This can be achieved in two ways: either by using a really wide moulding which might prove to be visually too dominant and expensive, or a fairly narrow moulding with an insert (or slide). Most inserts are fairly narrow and made of wood that can be

125

painted or covered in linen or velvet. The insert is simply an inner frame that visually increases the weight of the frame and provides a pleasing visual break between the painting and the outer frame.

Constructing an insert

Use a thin hard wood 2.5cm x 12mm(1in x ½in)with a 45° bevel on one edge (see fig. 5). Attach a ridge to the back underside edge of the insert (fig. 6) to provide an abutment when inserting the canvas. Sand the insert thoroughly and then paint with an acrylic gesso mixed to the desired colour for the insert. Use a fairly neutral colour—blue-grey, pink-grey, and so on, depending on the colours used in the painting. The corners should be mitred and glued.

Raw mouldings

Raw mouldings can be purchased from a local wood dealer and are usually in need of a thorough sanding before any decisions about surface treatment can be made. If they are of a good quality wood they can be stained with a transparent pigment. The most suitable solution would be a thinned acrylic paint such as raw umber, burnt umber, raw sienna, ochre or a mixture to achieve the desired colour. The fast drying acrylic paint will allow several coats of thin paint to be applied quickly. If you are dissatisfied with the matt result then a coat of varnish could be applied. This will enrich the grain. Here your experiments with gloss and matt varnish could be invaluable. If you are not happy with this procedure use a commercial wood stainer.

Many alternative finishes are possible. Having sealed the wood some exploration of stripping with a darker tone might prove useful. Plain emulsion paint finishes can be tried, or even high gloss lacquers. Gilded frames are always popular, and certainly not impossible to produce, but some specialized knowledge, perhaps the result of classes, will probably be necessary for satisfactory results.

Painting under glass

If you wish to frame an oil painting carried out on paper it is certainly worth while mounting it under glass. This entails mounting it on a cardboard mount before placing it behind the glass and frame. This is not quite as straightforward as it might seem. The important thing to remember with mounts is that the side widths should be the same or slightly smaller than the top width of cord, while the bottom width should be between a quarter and a third as large again. This is necessary to counter the optical illusion of the painting dropping out of the bottom of the mount if top and bottom are identical. Mounts under frames are traditionally cut with a bevelled edge. This is visually more attractive than a square-cut mount. The cardboard mount will slot into the inset area and be the same size as the glass. Knowing the overall size of the mount and the work to be placed behind it is all that is needed. Remember that the cut-out section of the mount must be slightly smaller than the painting to be mounted so as to provide an overlap for attaching the painting behind the mount. Choose the colour of the mount before cutting as changing the colour, although not impossible, will prove difficult with a fine bevelled edge exposed.

To cut a mount

Assume you have a cardboard mount 38cm x 30cm (15in x 12in) and a painting 33cm x 23cm (13in x 9in). You would need to cut a window in the mount slightly under the dimensions of the painting, that is 32cm x

The frame on the picture below is made in heavy metal to enhance the collage materials which include metal pieces on oil paint. The work is called Towards a Definitive Statement on the Coming Trends in Men's Wear and Accessories, *and is by Richard Hamilton.*

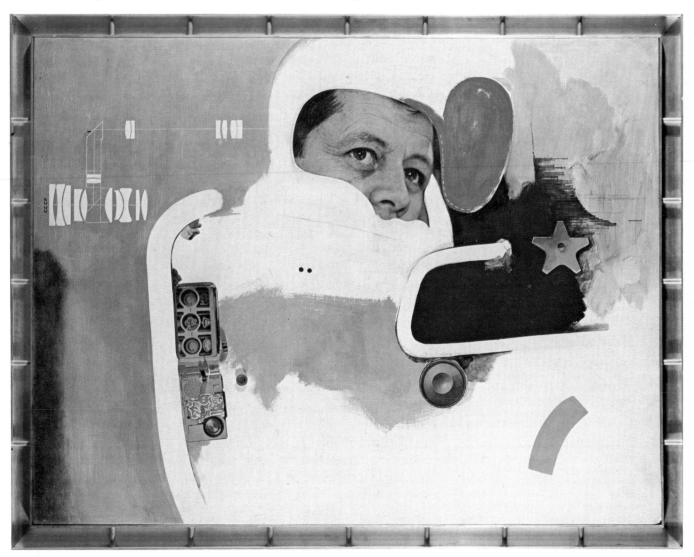

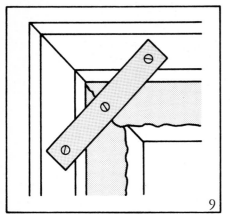

*Fig. 7 Using battens to make a
box-type frame.*
Fig. 8 Styles for batten framing.
*Fig. 9 Using a straight plate
to hold the canvas in place.*

22cm (12½in x 8½in) would be ideal, assuming you don't lose a critical part of the painting. On the length this would be 6cm (2¼in) of cardboard and on the width measurement just under 5.8cm (2⅛in). The side sections will be of 3cm (1⅛in) depth each, the top at least the same, but that would leave too large a base strip. About 3.3cm (1½in) against 4cm (1½in) would seem ideal. Draw out these measurements lightly on the top surface of the cardboard. For cutting the amount, use a very sharp craft knife or scalpel and a heavy metal ruler. Do not attempt to use a wooden ruler as the knife would cut into its edge should you falter while cutting. Place the cardboard on a cutting surface and align the ruler just inside the cutting line. Hold the knife at 45° against the ruler and cut from one corner to the other. Cut slowly and evenly without hesitating, and avoid overrunning the corner. If you are using really thick cardboard it may take two or three cuts. Repeat on the remaining sides. When these cuts are completed it is likely that the corners will still be slightly attached. Sever these by sliding the knife along to the corners, being sure to hold it at the same angle as the initial long cuts. Cut the final attachments. If cutting a mount with a bevel, again cut from front to back as a slight burring occurs on the back edge no matter how careful you may be. Attach the painting to the mount with clear adhesive tape then glue a sheet of thin cardboard of identical size onto the back of the mount to give additional protection. When the glue is dry, fix the mounted picture in the frame behind the glass with a few panel pins [picture nails], as for stretched canvas. Seal thoroughly to stop the possible infiltration of dust and dampness between glass and painting. Always make sure that the glass and mount are immaculately clean before final sealing.

By combining different widths of backing and adding decorative beading or other wooden trims, a variety of frames can be created. For example, a 12mm x 2.5cm (½in x 1in) batten attached first and set slightly back from the surface and then a 6mm x 3.5cm (¼in x 1¼in) batten fixed to it and projecting forward (fig. 7) would make an attractive box-type frame. The battens could be stained or painted different colours for added interest. Fig. 8 shows several possible combinations.

When making up the length for this type of frame, glue and clamp the pieces securely and be sure they are completely dry before nailing, otherwise they will split. Cut and fix corners as for moulding frames.

To secure the canvas in this type of frame use a straight plate across the corner (fig. 9) which will not only hold the canvas firmly in place but also reinforce the corner joint. One thing to remember, if you intend to use batten frames, is to be sure to carry the paint around the edge of the canvas so that no raw canvas will be left exposed.

Use a strong gummed paper strip to seal the area between the frame and the canvas.

Index